Better Homes and Gardens®

kitchen decorating ideas under $100

Meredith® Books
Des Moines, Iowa

Kitchen Decorating Ideas Under $100
Contributing Project Manager/Writer: Rebecca Jerdee
Contributing Graphic Designer: Matthew Eberhart, Evil Eye Design, Inc.
Copy Chief: Terri Fredrickson
Publishing Operations Manager: Karen Schirm
Senior Editor, Asset & Information Management: Phillip Morgan
Edit and Design Production Coordinator: Mary Lee Gavin
Editorial Assistant: Kaye Chabot
Book Production Managers: Pam Kvitne, Marjorie J. Schenkelberg, Rick von Holdt, Mark Weaver
Contributing Copy Editor: Ira Lacher
Contributing Proofreaders: Dan Degen, Nancy Ruhling, Susie Shupe
Contributing Cover Photographer: King Au
Contributing Indexer: Stephanie Reymann

Meredith® Books
Executive Director, Editorial: Gregory H. Kayko
Executive Director, Design: Matt Strelecki
Managing Editor: Amy Tincher-Durik
Senior Editor/Group Manager: Vicki Leigh Ingham
Marketing Product Manager: Steve Rogers

Publisher and Editor in Chief: James D. Blume
Editorial Director: Linda Raglan Cunningham
Excecutive Director, Marketing: Steve Malone
Executive Director, New Business Development: Todd M. Davis
Executive Director, Sales: Ken Zagor
Director, Operations: George A. Susral
Director, Production: Douglas M. Johnston
Director, Marketing: Amy Nichols
Business Director: Jim Leonard

Vice President and General Manager: Douglas J. Guendel

***Better Homes and Gardens®* Magazine**
Deputy Editor, Home Design: Oma Blaise Ford

Meredith Publishing Group
President: Jack Griffin
Executive Vice President: Bob Mate

Meredith Corporation
Chairman and Chief Executive Officer: William T. Kerr
President and Chief Operating Officer: Stephen M. Lacy

In Memoriam: E.T. Meredith III (1933–2003)

All of us at Meredith® Books are dedicated to providing you with information
and ideas to enhance your home. We welcome your comments and suggestions.
Write to us at: Meredith Books, Home Decorating and Design Editorial Department,
1716 Locust St., Des Moines, IA 50309-3023.

welcome

You'll love this book for its many approaches to updating and upgrading your kitchen on a budget. It will show you how to visually expand your kitchen spaces, give your cabinets a facelift, dress your windows, accent your walls, store provisions with style, or sit down to eat in a place you've styled for less than $100!

Turn these pages to give yourself a lift, find inspiration, and take action. It's all in your hands—and, of course, in the hands of great friends who help you. You'll find **doable projects** complete with **step-by-step instructions,** tips and techniques to boost your creative courage, and **ideas under $100** to tickle your imagination.

It's the cheapest kitchen **decorating fun** you'll ever have. So get on board, pick a page that reflects your personality, and unleash your creativity. Take doors off a cupboard to gain an open look. Freshen cabinetry with new hardware or a mosaic backsplash. Hang a vintage curtain or organize your crockery with style. Whatever your efforts—large or small—you'll be paid back with compliments, a sense of accomplishment, and a pocketful of **money saved.**

contents

52 accent

Give your kitchen walls or floors a visual boost with this collection of artistic projects and ideas. Will you love the chicken-print backsplash, the roses-are-pink-and-red backsplash, or the junkyard mosaic? Will you choose the patchwork wainscot, the spice-print wall, faux paneling, or the no-wrinkle rug? Or do you prefer the cheap-trick checkerboards, leaf backsplashes, and stamped surfaces?

68 store

Organize the contents of your cupboards with these storage styles: freestanding, open, closed, decorative, utilitarian, and personal. Cookbook libraries, kitchen islands, hanging racks, bargain shelving, baskets, portable caddies, and glass jars offer big-bang-for-the-buck options.

88 display

Pan for art by creating useful kitchen-utensil displays. Here are ways to turn beloved recipe cards, forks, pie tins, baking dishes, drawer pulls, candles, and dishes into treasured art objects.

106 eat

Order clever decorating ideas from this style menu. Choose from farmhouse, romantic, island, flea market, blue and white, build-it-yourself, or no-sew styles. Finish with pinstriped chair slipcovers, crackle-finished furniture, or fabrics decorated with iron-on slogans.

OPEN to gain space

Expect more from your kitchen than any other room in the house—it's the action zone and heart of your home.

Want it to live bigger and better for less? The photographs on the following pages show you how to visually expand and physically free up your spaces. For less than $100 an idea, you can uncover the hidden potential within your kitchen and raise its levels of usefulness and comfort.

expand your kitchen for less

Use these tips to lighten and lift the look of your kitchen:

▌ **Paint woodwork white** to outline and visually enlarge the architecture. Choose high-grade paints. They are simple to apply, cover beautifully, and last longer, saving you money in the long run. With routine care, newly painted surfaces can last up to 10 years.

▌ **Remove kitchen doors,** if they aren't needed for privacy, to create an easier traffic flow and cut away awkward barriers.

▌ **Avoid patterned wallcoverings** and busy borders that add visual clutter.

▌ **Paint a white band** along the top of the wall to connect with the ceiling and visually lift the room. A 12-inch-wide band is about the right size.

▌ **Install light-color laminate flooring** as a substitute for natural wood or dark vinyl flooring. It can be applied quickly and is exceptionally easy to maintain.

▌ **Fasten beveled mirror panels** at the backs of open cupboards to reflect light. The panels also give shelves the illusion of expanded depth.

OPEN UP. Replace a kitchen door with a pair of swinging shutters that requires less clearance than a full-size door.

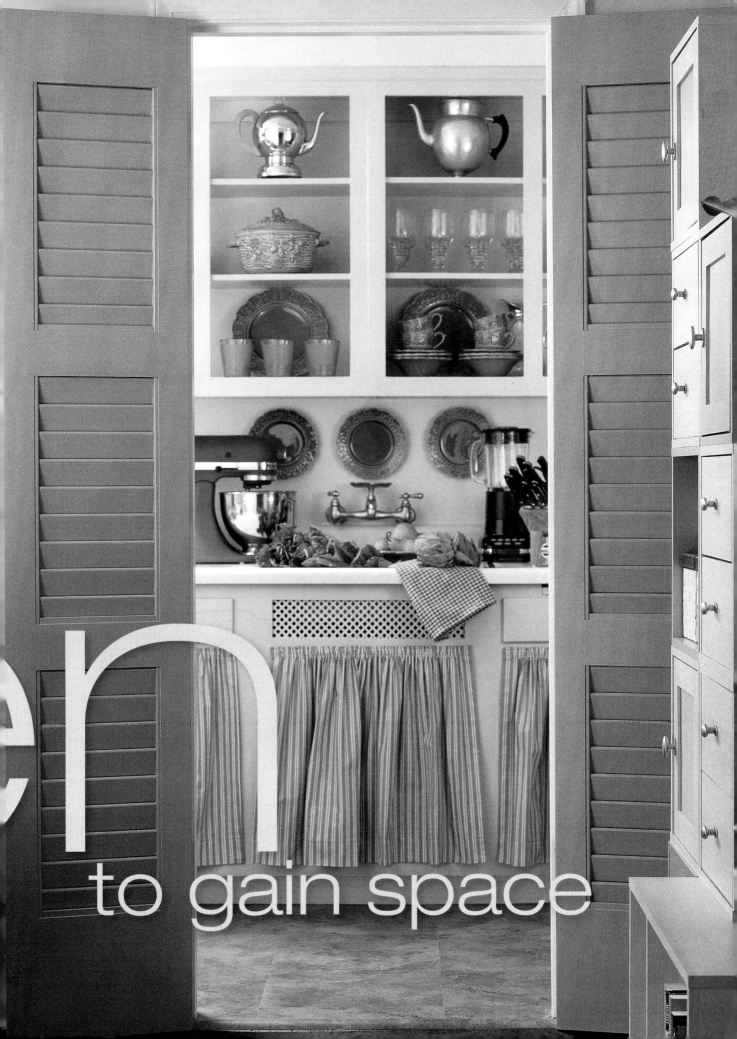

en
to gain space

thrifty cabinet treatments

Removing cabinet doors is less expensive than replacing them. Another advantage: Door removal visually widens the spaces of a narrow kitchen. Here are some ideas for treating the interiors of open cupboards:

▮ **Remove doors** and fill in holes with wood filler. Sand until smooth, and paint or stain as desired. If you plan an applied interior treatment such as wallcovering, prime the interior walls of the cupboard where the covering will be applied.

▮ **Remember wrapping schoolbooks** in craft paper? Line open shelves with 22-gauge scraps of galvanized sheet metal to add shine and a stainless-steel look to your kitchen. Locate a local sheet metal fabricator to purchase material. First cut shelf liners with tin snips. Wearing gloves, fold the metal over the shelf fronts, press with your fingertips, and glue the liners securely in place with construction glue. To coordinate with nearby drawers, apply the same wrapping principles over drawer fronts. When the metal is securely wrapped in place, return the hardware to the original holes.

▮ **Enclose laundry appliances** in or near your kitchen with off-the-rack shower curtains hung on cables or curtain rods. This softens the hard edges of a kitchen and avoids swinging doors that get in the way.

▮ **For reversible looks** at the backs of open cupboards, cut ¼-inch plywood inserts the size of the cupboard backs. Paint one side of each insert with a color that contrasts with the rest of the cupboard. Decoupage the other side with map sections or pieces of wallcovering. Set the inserts at the back of the cupboard openings. To change the scene, flip them around.

CUPBOARD ACCENTS. *Remove upper cabinet doors to give a narrow kitchen a sense of wideness. Then set off the revealed shelves with a decorative treatment.*

Be discriminating about which doors you remove from your cupboards for decorative purposes. Avoid removing doors that hide clutter. Once the interior of a cabinet or cupboard is opened, it becomes part of the room's overall decor.

FACELIFT. For a crisp, streamlined look, remove a few doors and eliminate the window cornice from builder's-grade cupboards. Paint worn wood an energizing coat of white.

lights & mirrors

Combine natural light, artificial light, and mirrors for maximum openness and illumination of your kitchen.

natural light

Natural light is optimal light. To achieve good natural light control during the day, hang minimal window treatments, such as plantation shutters, inside-mount miniblinds, or a classic white roller shade that disappears behind a valance.

mirrors

Mirror panels inserted at the backs of open cupboards work magic by doubling the light they reflect and creating the illusion of deeper spaces.

FOOL THE EYE. *A mirror hung on a standard-issue door gives this tiny kitchen a deeper view as well as a faux French look.*

TAPE IT. *Fasten mullions to the mirror with small pieces of evenly spaced double-stick cushion tape.*

CLIP IT. *Plastic mirror clips hold the mirror in place on the door.*

not-so-natural light

▮ **Pendants.** From incandescent bulbs with vintage glass shades to ultra-futuristic halogen cones that pack brightness into tiny fixtures, hanging pendants are popular for ceiling fixtures. Place pendants over an island or countertop where low-hanging fixtures don't interfere with traffic flow.

▮ **Tube lights** (miniature white lights in plastic channels) are easy to use in coves above cabinetry. Simply plug them in and lay them across the tops of the cabinets.

▮ **Uplights or sconces** play up the nonstandard features of architecturally interesting ceilings.

▮ **Downlights or recessed fixtures** light the kitchen in a general way, supplemented by task lights.

▮ **Strip lights** under cabinets and shelves light tasks on the counter or accent a display of dishes in a freestanding cupboard.

▮ **Tracks** with movable fixtures provide general light or may be used to accent specific areas.

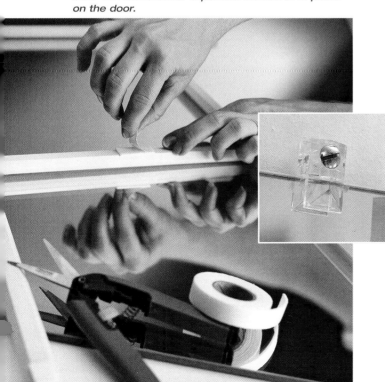

HOW TO
create a mirrored door

1. **Gather** a mirror (have a home center cut a size that leaves a 6-inch border of door), a prefabricated window mullion, double-stick cushion tape, and four mirror clips.
2. **Trim** the prefabricated window mullion panel to size with a miter or circular saw so the ends align with the outside measurements of the mirror.
3. **Adhere** the mullions to the mirror with small pieces of evenly spaced double-stick cushion tape.
4. **Mount** the mirror onto the door using four mirror clips, placing them about 3 inches in from each corner on the top and bottom.

makeover on a low budget

When cash is short and it's worth your time, take these steps for a kitchen facelift:

▌▌ **A new coat of paint** is a cost-effective way to make your kitchen spaces feel more expansive and imbue them with freshness and cleanliness. A little prep work makes the results long-lasting, so prepare your walls and cabinetry before painting. To determine which type of paint is on the cabinets or walls, apply rubbing alcohol to a clean rag and wipe an inside surface of a cabinet and the surface of a wall. If paint comes up, it's latex (water base); if the paint is unaffected, it's alkyd (oil base). You can paint oil over latex. However, only certain latex paints will adhere to oils, so check the label before you buy. Thoroughly clean cabinets and walls to remove dirt and cooking grease.

▌▌ **Replacing doors and drawer fronts** transforms the look for much less than the cost of a complete remodeling. Because most built-in cabinets are produced in standard dimensions, you can easily replace old doors with new ones. A less expensive option: fresh paint on doors and cupboard frames. White cupboards and cabinets look best with white appliances and have a unified, clean, modern look.

▌▌ **Think of hardware** as kitchen jewelry. Add new metal accents to highlight a resurfaced kitchen cabinet. Metals—gold, brass, silver, stainless steel, galvanized tin, nickel, or chrome—work wonders to highlight cupboard doors and fixtures. Furniture or lighting fixtures may have shiny metal parts too. A good rule: Choose one metal for the scheme and, as much as possible, stick to it when adding hardware.

INTERIOR SEDUCTION. All that glitters is not gold. It could be the sunlight reflecting off narrow mirror panels laid along the back walls of a cupboard. Mirror panels invite the eye inside and add light to the depth of open cupboards.

PANELING THAT ISN'T. Create the look of paneling for the price of moldings: Apply white-painted wood moldings over wallboard. For the horizontal ledge, attach undercap molding to the wall 20 inches below the ceiling and top it with doorstop molding. For the vertical bands, attach screen molding strips, spacing them 24 inches apart.

cupboard
with a view

Bring architectural interest and more storage to your kitchen by adding a cabinet in front of the window. Removing the cabinet back panel and replacing the cabinet doors with glass panels allow light to travel through the cabinet. For more character, top the cabinets with crown molding. A glass ledge suspended by steel cables (available at home-improvement centers) adds still more storage. A glass dealer can cut the glass to size and drill holes for the cables. Metal crimps fasten the looped cable ends under the ledge.

HOW TO
install this cabinet

1. **Measure** for and buy a cabinet to fit between the two cabinets flanking your kitchen window.
2. **Remove** the back panel from the cabinet to let the sunlight shine through.
3. **Hang** the cabinet slightly higher than the flanking cabinetry to vary heights and to allow for window operation.
4. **Replace** the recessed wooden panels on the cabinet doors with grooved glass panels.
5. **Top** the cabinets with crown molding.

SINK WINDOW VIEW. A glass-door cabinet above the window provides storage without spoiling the view. The glass panels diffuse the light and let glassware colors show.

LESS IS MORE.
Cope with damaged or sticking lower cabinet doors by removing them. Easy-open pull-out baskets add function and charm.

BETWEEN STUDS (OPPOSITE).
Carve out storage racks between wall studs. These trays rest in a tall catchall.

SHELF LIFE (BELOW). *This trio of wood shelves supported by curving brackets gains old-fashioned flair on a wall covered with beaded board.*

shelf esteem

▌**Display only a few objects** on open shelves for a casual look.

▌**A one-color display** of dishes creates a more expansive, simple look than a multitude of colors.

▌**Before you install** display cabinets, measure your collectibles so your shelves are the right distances apart for a perfect fit.

▌**Glass shelves** take up little room and almost disappear in the visual scheme of things. A good place to hang shelves is in front of a window, where they can hold a few live plants.

▌**For a clean, up-to-date look,** use white paint and white dishes on open shelves. Then accent the arrangement with a white pitcher filled with fresh flowers in one bright color.

REVIVE cabinet faces

Some kitchens require total reconstruction. Others function perfectly, needing little more than a cosmetic lift. If your kitchen is only 20 or 30 years old and in good shape and working condition, give your outdated cabinets surface treatments to erase that tired look.

Look through this chapter to find ways to rejuvenate your kitchen cabinets with paint, stain, fabric, wood, wire, and hardware. The happiest part of surface treatments is their economy.

skin-deep beauty

One way to add instant character to your kitchen is by displaying architectural elements. From worn gingorbroad trim to iron fencing, these items dramatize decor. Scour salvage yards, auctions, construction sites, or antiques stores for pieces that catch your eye.

▮ **Peeling paint and spots of rust** are part of what makes these pieces distinctive. You can find inexpensive reproductions of salvage items at import stores and home centers for under $100.

▮ **An important element of style** is the juxtaposition of contrasting textures, such as the cool sleek island, *opposite,* and the warm rusty iron gate hung in front of it. Combine smooth with rough, shiny with matte, or thick with thin to engage your senses of sight and touch.

GIVE IT CHARACTER. *A weathered iron gate brings intriguing texture to a standard white paneled island in this kitchen, altering the mood from modern to country.*

live

cabinet faces

paint and save

Paint in a can is like a genie in a bottle: It's at your every command. Beyond that, it's liquid gold in the decorating bank. For just a few dollars and a little time, paint rewards you with many decorating returns. Here are some moods you can express with paint:

▌ **Neutral & serene.** Grant your wish for a quiet, calm, yet strong kitchen space by painting it with taupes, browns, grays, and whites. For drama, use light and dark neutrals. Two shades of the same color provide a soft, subtle look.

▌ **Cool & restful.** Blues and greens are associated with peace and serenity. Light versions (tints) open kitchens, keeping their moods airy and fresh. Dark blues and greens (shades) give kitchens weight, drama, and depth. Grayed blues and greens work as neutrals. Paint the ceiling a close or matching color to wrap the room with the mood.

▌ **Warm & vivacious.** Some like it hot. If that's your style, paint your kitchen with bold reds and yellows. Be careful, though: Large expanses of intense or saturated versions of these warm colors can wear you out. To use intense reds or oranges successfully, paint only one wall as an accent. Or use a brilliant hue on the cabinet interiors to give a color jolt.

COLOR 1-2-3. Take cabinets from boring to brilliant with a good sanding and washes of stain in three colors. Complete the look with retro-style brushed-chrome hardware.

If ink and crayon marks or water stains mar the surfaces you plan to paint, cover them with a stain-blocking primer (available at paint stores) before painting. This prevents marks from bleeding through the finished coat of paint.

SPICE IT UP. Cabinets get a zesty paint combo of paprika and saffron. Hardware and a modern but nostalgic skirt, suspended from a steel cable under the sink, complete the facelift.

one facelift
two ways

Compare these do-it-my-way makeovers accomplished on standard cabinetry. Do they strike a creative chord for a cabinet facelift of your own?

HOW TO
decorate for classic beauty

1. **Gather** primer, red and white paints, brushes, red and white toile curtains, and brushed-chrome hardware pulls.
2. **Freshen exteriors** of cabinets with white paint. Paint interiors of glass-door cabinets red to provide a dramatic backdrop for dishware.
3. **Hang** red and white toile cafe curtains to coordinate with red and white dishware.
4. **Arrange** red and white dishes in glass-door cupboards to complete the color theme.
5. **Replace** old hardware with brushed-chrome hardware to add polish.

NEW TRADITIONAL (OPPOSITE). *Clever additions of bun feet, beaded board, and glass-panel doors give standard oak cabinetry the look of freestanding furniture. The original wood finish is covered with white paint for an updated classic look.*

OLD MADE OLDER (ABOVE). *The same architectural additions of bun feet, beaded board, and glass-panel doors are applied to a second set of cabinetry but treated differently with old-fashioned paint-and-stain finishes and patterned wallcovering.*

HOW **TO**

create an antique look

1. **Gather** cleaning agent, sandpaper, primer, black or ivory paint, dark brown stain, a tack cloth, and polyurethane.
2. **Wash** the cabinets thoroughly. Sand to ensure a good bond between the old finish and new paint.
3. **Apply** primer to all surfaces. Paint the cabinets black or ivory as desired. Let the paint dry overnight.
4. **Sand** the cabinets lightly to distress them, paying special attention to the edges. Wipe clean with a tack cloth.
5. **Brush** on a thin coat of dark brown stain. Wipe away most of it with a rag, leaving more in corners and crevices.
6. **Apply** several coats of polyurethane to protect the finish and make cleaning easier.

fabric world

The soft textures and patterns of fabrics pleasantly contrast with a kitchen's hard edges and utilitarian looks. Fabric at the windows or on a table, or skirts that replace cabinet doors are ways to effectively bring pattern and print personality into your cooking and eating spaces. Another benefit? Fabrics by the yard or garage sale buys are easy on the budget.

▌**Choose muslin and canvas fabrics** to create low-cost style. In spite of their humble prices and plainness, they take on an elegant appearance when paired with white paints and natural surfaces.

▌**Mix old and new patterns and prints.** Any fabric can come into decorative play provided it's in good condition and carries the attitude you crave. Besides a consistent color scheme, the secret to mixing and matching fabrics is scale. For the simplest way to mix fabrics, select a showcase print (table covering, for example) and coordinate it with striped cabinet skirts or plaid door panels in the same colors. Then add cafe curtains in a coordinating print with midsize motifs.

SHIRRED PANELS. *If recessed-panel doors are warped or damaged, salvage them with fabric. Remove the panels, sand the frames, and paint them. Then, install shirred fabric panels on the inside of the cabinet doors, using curtain rods available at any home center.*

SKIRT FLIRT (LEFT). These 1950s metal cabinets below the sink had dented doors. A skirt made from two dish towels attached with hook-and-loop fastening tape replaced them. Colorful vintage earrings are clipped or hot-glued onto the edge of one of the towels.

COVER-UP (BELOW). Hide cleansers under your sink with a pleated curtain that's an eye-catching decorative statement. Attached with hook-and-loop tape or hung from a wire, these panels can be as subdued or attention-getting as you like.

stencil it for pennies

Visit a crafts supply store to gather stenciling materials and tools to beautify your cabinetry. First leaf through the displays of plastic stencils to choose your favorite. You'll find a range of large and small floral stencils, animals, leaf motifs, and geometrics. If you are a beginner at stenciling, choose a simple motif that requires only one color, such as the white stencils on blue cabinetry in the photograph on this page. Then move to the paint racks to select a color. Color is a personal choice, but for a little guidance refer to page 20 to read about moods created by certain colors. You'll also need a stenciling brush and a spray adhesive that allows you to temporarily attach the stencil to the surface while you work.

 HOT **TIP**

Are you a stenciling novice? If so you may want to practice on some smaller surfaces, such as butcher paper or large cardboard, before you tackle the cabinetry in your kitchen. The backs of cabinet doors also are good candidates for your warm-ups.

 HOW **TO**

stencil a cabinet

1. **Gather** sandpaper, tack cloth, sponge, primer, cabinetry paint, stencil, stencil adhesive, acrylic paint, paintbrushes, stencil brush, and polyurethane.
2. **Remove** the cabinet doors, drawers, and hardware. Sand the surfaces to be painted and wipe clean with a tack cloth. Apply primer and let dry. Paint surfaces in the desired color.
3. **Spray** each stencil with stencil adhesive, as needed, and press it in place onto the cabinet door or drawer front.
4. **Stencil** the motifs with acrylic paint and a stencil brush, applying the paint with short, rapid, pouncing motions. Clean the stencils with water and a sponge frequently to avoid paint buildup.
5. **Apply** several coats of water-base polyurethane over the painted surfaces to protect the finish and make cleaning easier.
6. **Attach** the hardware, rehang the cabinet doors, and replace the drawers.

FANCY THIS. In such a pretty kitchen, microwaving frozen dinners feels like fairy-tale cooking. Paint the cabinets a pale blue and stencil on a pattern you found at a crafts supply store.

update with hardware

Your cabinetry's handles, hinges, and doorknobs are the final touches and style setters for the space. Choose them carefully.

▌ **So what's your style?** Antique, contemporary, cottage, or country? Eclectic, European, farmhouse, or Asian? Or how about tropical, urban, vintage, or whimsical? When you decide to purchase your new hardware, keep your style in mind because you'll be faced with a great number of choices.

▌ **If you plan to fit your new hardware** into the holes left by the old hardware, you may find your choices more limited than if you were to fill in old holes and refinish the cabinetry. All hardware isn't standard. Take some samples of the old hardware when you shop.

▌ **The most affordable places to shop** are home centers and hardware stores where you can choose from racks of common choices or special-order hardware for a custom look. But don't overlook garage sales, flea markets, and antiques stores. Or surf the Internet by typing in "kitchen cabinet hardware" on a search engine.

▌ **Give your cabinet doors and drawers a good cleaning** before hanging new hardware. Or freshen them witih paint or stain so the new hardware will show to the best advantage.

Count the number of doorknobs, handles, or drawer pulls before heading out to stores, garage sales, or flea markets. You don't want to be caught empty-handed when you get to the last door or drawer.

OUTLINED EMBELLISHMENT. A simple stroke of red paint adds dimension to kitchen drawers and brings attention to new, shapely hardware. Use a stiff brush to add a dry-brush stroke of black paint around the perimeter of the red bands.

get wired

If you're a hands-on original who thinks outside the box, one of these cabinet facelifts may appeal to you. You'll need basic tools, safety goggles, and a pair of gloves to protect your hands from sharp wire ends.

HOW TO
insert hardware cloth or chicken wire

1. **Gather** sandpaper, primer, hardware cloth or chicken wire, paint or stain, and brushes.
2. **Cut out** the recessed panels from cabinet doors close to the rails with a saber saw. Turn the doors over to pry out remaining wood with pliers.
3. **Sand and prime** the drawers and cabinet doors. Give them the desired painted or stained finish before applying the hardware cloth inserts.
4. **Using heavy-duty shears,** cut the cloth or wire 2 inches larger than door openings on all sides.
5. **Attach** the hardware cloth or chicken wire panels to the backs of the cabinet doors with heavy-duty staples and a sturdy staple gun.
6. **Cover** the raw edges of the hardware cloth with thin strips of wood painted or stained to match the cabinet doors.

INDUSTRIAL CHIC (OPPOSITE) meets junk-market country with this novel facelift. Resurfacing the door fronts with hardware cloth also adds up to a bargain-style cosmetic treatment.

CHICKEN WIRE CHIC (BELOW). No-frills chicken wire flies the coop to give this kitchen cabinet a surprising makeover. Pastoral pink toile fabric fastened behind the chicken wire creates a homespun cottage style. For a more casual and airy look, leave out the fabric and let the chicken wire go solo.

FLOUR   OATS   SUGAR

make it memorable

When your kitchen refurbishing goals are modest (a fresh look without a major investment), choose one of these quick, decorative cabinet renovations.

▌ **To turn heads,** turn the pages of family albums for pictures to display on a few carefully selected cabinet doors. For an antique look, have a copy center enlarge small pictures to the desired sizes in black and white. Or enlarge them yourself. Most copy centers have self-serve machines. If you have a scanner, color printer, and computer, you can make your own prints. Fasten the prints to painted cupboard doors with matte acrylic medium or decoupage glue.

▌ **For architecture that stands out,** replace boring, characterless doors with more interesting ones from salvage yards and shops. Carry a tape measure while you shop so you'll get the correct height, width, and thickness. While you're at it, pick up salvage doorknobs that are thrilling to the touch and add more personality to your new (old) doors.

REJUVENATE (OPPOSITE). Old white laminate cabinets were brought back to life with grassy-green paint and embellishments. Wood veneers were applied to the center panels of some doors, while others were fitted with translucent glass inserts held by mahogany frames. Another door holds matted family photos.

CHALK IT UP (LEFT). This chalkboard-in-a-cabinet makes prime use of a kitchen work zone to help busy families stay connected. Paint the recessed panel of a cabinet with chalkboard paint (available at home centers and paint stores) and add a ledge for blackboard chalk and an eraser.

TREAT your windows

Window treatments, like fashion, have gone casual. Formal swags, expensive brocades, and puffed-up balloon shades are being replaced by clean lines and simple elegance. Is it any wonder? Who has time or money for all that drama and expense?

The true benefit of the recent window-dressing-down revolution is a carefree attitude toward decorating that results in fresh and inexpensive window treatments. This chapter contains do-it-yourself ideas for over-the-sink windows as well as larger windows in the eating areas of your kitchen.

inexpensive & easy window dressings

▌Vintage tablecloths, kitchen towels, and napkins weren't made to be window treatments. But today everyone sees the advantages of adapting them to their panes: You can buy them for bargain prices and hang up the delightful patterns and colors of another era.

▌Miniblinds make versatile window coverings because you easily can adjust them to let in as much or as little light as desired. They're affordable options with several finishes and materials. For example, white wood slats create a classic look while wood slats offer an informal, relaxed feel to a space. Metallic blades promise a clean, contemporary look.

▌A Roman blind provides a minimalist, light-friendly window treatment. Hang it above a recessed window so it can be raised and lowered without brushing an arrangement of plants on the sill.

▌Tab-tops, a favorite, are lightweight, casual, and carefree ways to soften the hard edges of window frames.

▌Curtains with valances, although not as practical as easy-to-clean blinds, give windows a softer look. Turn your window into a focal point by framing it with a gathered style in colorful fabric.

CLIP ART. Vintage toile on clip rings becomes a curtain. Linen bath towels are layered as a tabletop display to coordinate with the window.

at
your windows

toss in the towel

Tea towels make excellent no-sew curtains when you hinge them together with fusible-adhesive tape. Style-wise, tea-towel curtains emphasize a laid-back, countrified character or a '30s, '40s, or '50s atmosphere. Hung cafe style over the lower half of the window, a towel curtain, especially if it's light in color, provides privacy without blocking out much light.

▌**For an attractive fullness** on a gathered or shirred towel curtain, measure the width of the window and multiply that number by two. Collect enough towels to make this measurement.

▌**For pleasing lengths**, allowing for curtain tabs, measure from the top of the rod to the sill. Hang cafe-style rods directly in front of the lower sash. Three-quarter-length towels can hang on tension rods set inside the window frame at almost any height. If the window has mullions, line up the curtain rod with a mullion for simplicity or let the length of the towel guide placement *(opposite)*.

WINDOW WEAR. *For cafe curtains, fold tops of vintage towels over so bottoms just skim the windowsill. Sew or fuse the folded layers to create a casing. Attach buttons across the seam and thread a curtain rod through the casing.*

When fusing fabric layers, placing a paper towel between the fabric and your iron protects your iron from the edges of sticky fusible-adhesive material that may escape from under fabric.

BUTTONED UP (LEFT). *Transform cloth napkins into pretty curtains. You'll need two to four napkins per panel, depending on the size of your window. Fold under 3 inches of the top of the napkin to create a rod pocket. Sew on five evenly spaced buttons, sewing through both layers of fabric to secure the rod pocket. Pin a napkin to the bottom of the first one, overlapping it three inches. Attach the two napkins with five more buttons. Repeat for each panel until you reach the desired length.*

EMBROIDERED TOWELS (OPPOSITE). *Cut embroidered towels to allow maximum use of the designs and stitch the towel panels together to form each curtain. Sew bias tape along the top and bottom edges of the curtain to hem; add tabs made from the same tape.*

plate rail topper

Provide a display opportunity on high by topping a window frame with a narrow strip of molding and a mini shelf. For a fancy finish, run glass drawer knobs along the width of the frame and hang a valance.

cheap thrills

The fun of this project is collecting antique drawer pulls. Find glass drawer pulls that screw through the front; look for them in the hardware sections of salvage stores and at specialty stalls of large flea markets. Or use double-ended screws to mount drawer pulls that screw in from the back.

Mix and match styles of drawer pulls but limit your purchases to those made with glass. If you prefer drawer pulls of another material, such as brass or iron, keep the look unified by sticking with one metal and not mixing in those made with glass.

HOW TO

make this plate rail

1. **Gather** a 1×4 board cut slightly wider than your window frame (plate ledge), picture-frame and dentil moldings 10 inches longer than the 1×4, sandpaper, primer, white latex paint, 6d finishing nails, screws, No. 16×1-inch brads, and glass drawer pulls.
2. **Rout** a plate-holding groove ¼-inch wide and ¼-inch deep in the 1×4. Miter picture-frame molding to cap the front and ends of the 1×4. Miter dentil molding to hide the seam between the top of the window frame and the plate rail; set aside.
3. **Apply** a primer coat to the boards. Let dry. Sand lightly and apply one or two coats of latex paint.
4. **Attach** the picture-frame molding to the 1×4 with 6d finishing nails. Screw through the 1×4 to attach to the top of the window frame. Use brads to attach the dentil molding and conceal the seam between the plate rail and window frame.
5. **Space** glass drawer pulls evenly along the top face of the window frame as pegs for a tie-top valance.

WELCOME SUNNY DAYS (OPPOSITE).
Light- and privacy-controlling shutters let the sun in. Hinge half-height shutters inside the window frame. Stitch dotted Swiss fabric with a scalloped edge into a summery spaghetti-strap valance. Loop the straps over drawer pulls on the window frame.

choosing curtains

The right window treatment can transform a flawed kitchen space into a place that reflects your style and your sense of beauty. It can highlight your kitchen's best qualities or turn problem eating areas into sleek, sophisticated spaces. Before you choose a window treatment, consider:

❚❚ Needs for privacy and energy control. A gauzy scarf swag may be beautiful, but you may need a shade beneath it for better insulation and shelter from the eyes of passersby.

❚❚ The amount of light you want through your windows. If privacy isn't an issue, choose top treatments, such as a simple valance or cornice without blinds or undermount curtains.

❚❚ Traffic patterns. Puddles of silk flowing from a dining room window add great drama but wouldn't be practical on a kitchen's sliding glass door to the patio.

❚❚ Wall, floor, cupboard, and appliance colors. Curtain colors should coordinate with the rest of the room.

❚❚ Expense. Consider thrifty miniblinds and shades for strictly functional windows and sew simple curtains to save money.

HOT TIP

Kitchen window treatments usually need more frequent washing than those in other rooms. Choose blinds or curtains that are easy to remove and replace.

HOW TO

make these curtains

1. **Purchase** four swing-arm rods. Choose a fabric, such as a loosely woven linen, that ravels easily. (For correct amounts read Step 2, below.) Make sure the grain is straight. If you don't know how to check for this, ask a fabric store employee.
2. **Mount** swing-arm rods at the tops and bottoms of the windows. To determine the length of the panel, measure the distance between the top and bottom rods and add 12 inches. For the width of the fabric panel, use the measurement of the length of the rod plus 2 inches.
3. **Make** a mark 6 inches in from each short end of the fabric and ravel the fabric until the resulting fringe reaches the mark. Hem the long sides with ½-inch rolled hems.
4. **Tie** the fringe around top rods: Divide the raveled fabric ends into clusters about ¼ inch wide. Divide each cluster into two equal strands and tie them around the rods, placing the rod close to the fabric edge. Repeat for the bottom rods.
5. **Adjust** the knots and trim the fringed ends to an even length.

FRAY AWAY. Fringed-linen panels are mounted on swing-arm rods to create this classic window treatment. Sunlight illuminates the linen texture, while the hand-raveled fringe adds a rustic touch.

shelves with a view

A glass shelf isn't the first thing that comes to mind for a window treatment. But here are some of its benefits:

▌ **Blurring the boundaries** between inside and the out-of-doors is a trend. Bring the sky, the sun, and the garden in by way of a few exposed panes. You'll take the tedium out of kitchen chores by taking in the outdoor panorama.

▌ **Letting in maximum light**, especially on the northern side of the house, is wise. Light deprivation makes chores feel more like chores. Natural light coming through windows lifts your mood and gives the kitchen an open, spacious look. See Chapter 1 for more ideas on openness.

▌ **Softening the hard edges** of a window frame with plant textures and a variety of natural greens is an inexpensive design solution. Set pots on shelves or line a shelf with a cut-flower or green display such as the one shown on page 93.

HOW TO
install a glass shelf

1. **Gather** drywall anchors, shelf brackets, a green-tinted glass shelf in the desired size, and plastic desk buttons.
2. **Use drywall anchors** to fasten brackets outside the window trim to be sure your window remains operable. Measure the distance between the brackets before ordering the shelf.
3. **Have a glazier** cut glass to your specifications. For displaying lightweight items, ¼-inch-thick shelves will suffice. Heavier objects, such as potted plants, may require ½-inch-thick glass. Choose seamed shelf edges, which have been smoothed for easy handling, or slightly more expensive polished edges, which are rounded to reveal the green tint of the glass.
4. **Place plastic desk buttons** where glass meets bracket, to avoid scratching the glass. If desired, use double-stick clear glazing tape to firmly attach the shelves to the brackets.

OUTSIDE IN (OPPOSITE). This long glass shelf is a clever and efficient solution for displaying collectibles and houseplants that look best in the light. Curtains, shirred top and bottom, complement the shelf while providing privacy.

penny-wise details, priceless charm

With the more casual style of today's window treatments, you can indulge your imagination when choosing hanging devices. Consider these notions:

▌Clips. Hang scarves, table coverings, napkins, or lengths of simply hemmed fabric quickly and easily with clip-on curtain rings you can find in curtain departments. Experiment with rustic clothespins for a country look or snap fabric lengths to large office clips over rods for utility chic.

▌Hooks. To hang tab-top curtains from window frames and walls, use wall hooks, boat cleats, Shaker pegs, door pulls, shank buttons, and even earrings.

▌Loops. Hang curtains with rope, rattail cording, or ribbon looped through grommets and buttonholes.

▌Special effects. Add an unexpected bit of magic by hanging a string of white mini-lights over a rod that holds a pair of curtain panels.

▌Rods. Be inventive. Instead of hanging curtains on standard rods, try bamboo poles, cable wire, hardware store threaded rod, peg board, PVC or copper piping, or a tree branch.

HAVE A BALL *Ball finials on this curtain rod are covered by hemmed circles of matching gingham check fabric. Gimp ties the covers in place.*

HOW TO

buckle up a ready-made curtain panel

1. **Gather** a ready-made curtain, tab fabric, and overall clasps. Amounts vary by curtain size.
2. **For one tab:** Cut a 10½x3½-inch piece of fabric. Fold it in half lengthwise, right sides facing. Sew along the long edge, using a ¼-inch seam allowance, to form a tube; turn right side out and press. Turn raw edges of each open end inside the tab about ¼ inch; sew along each end.
3. **Position one end** of the tab at the top of the curtain on the back, about 1 inch in from the side and with ½ inch of the tab end overlapping the curtain; stitch in place. Sew the button of a clasp to the front of the curtain and corresponding tab about 1½ inches below the top edge of the curtain. Thread the clasp onto the tab. Repeat, placing tabs evenly across the curtain; end with the last tab 1 inch in from the side. With thread, fasten tabs at equal lengths in clasps; slip them over the rod.

BUCKLE UP (LEFT). *For a country cottage look, hang ready-made curtain panels from clasps used for making overalls.*

FLATWARE FANCIES (OPPOSITE). *There's no greasy spoon at this cafe curtain. Silverware with handles bent back holds curtains on a rod.*

create a new tab-top

For fun that transforms standard tab-top curtains into window dressings with personality, try one of these ideas.

KNOTTY BUT NICE. *Hand-stitched tab-tops tied into square-shape knots put ready-made panels in the spotlight.*

HOW TO
make knotted tab-tops

1. **Gather** a ready-made curtain, coordinating fabric (fabric ties), pins, and thread.
2. **For one tab,** cut a 10×3½-inch piece of coordinating fabric. Fold it in half lengthwise, right sides facing. Machine-stitch along the long edge, using a ½-inch seam allowance, to form a tube; turn right side out and press, with the seam along one side. Turn raw edges of each open end inside the tab about ¼ inch; machine-stitch each end. Fold the tube in half, matching ends, to create the tab. Position the tab at the top of the panel front, 1 inch from the side edge with ½ inch of the ends overlapping the curtain panel; pin and sew.
3. **For one tie,** cut a 27½×3½-inch piece of the same coordinating fabric. Sew to form a tube; turn right side out, and finish raw edges, as for the tabs. Fold the tie in half crosswise to find the midpoint; center and pin the midpoint on the front of the tab, perpendicular to the tab and just below the top edge of the curtain panel. Sew a ½-inch square in the middle of the tie, securing it to the tab and panel. Tie in a square-shape knot.
4. **Repeat,** positioning the desired number of tabs evenly and placing the last tab 1 inch from the opposite side. To hang, feed them over the rod.

VALANCING ACT. *When there's no call for a full-length panel, here's a tab-top look that simply swags across the top of the window. Although it looks as though it's one long piece, this treatment is really a series of double-sided oblong sections tied together over the rod with jute.*

HOW **TO**

make the jute loops valance

1. **Gather** a curtain rod, thread, jute twine, and three yards each of two coordinating swag fabrics. This will make four swags to cover a 40-inch-wide window; adjust amounts for other window sizes.

2. **For one swag,** cut one 16×48-inch piece from each fabric. Measure, mark, and cut off each corner of each piece to form elongated octagons.

3. **Sew the two fabrics** together (right sides facing and using ¼-inch seams), leaving an opening for turning. Turn, press, and sew the opening closed. Repeat to make three more swags.

4. **To hang the swags,** lay a panel flat, front side up, and lay another panel, front side up, on top of it, matching all edges. Beginning at the center of the rod, loop one end of the pair over the rod from the back with the front side of the fabric against the rod, so about 10 inches of fabric hangs over the front of the rod, revealing the lining fabric. Use jute twine directly under the rod to cinch this front section to the remaining lengths of swag. Separate the remaining portions of the two panels and pull one to each side of the cinched tie with the front fabric facing. Match up one of the free ends with the end of a new panel, loop over the rod, and cinch as before. Repeat until you reach rod ends.

roll-up shades

Clean and neat, roll-up blinds and shades are a classic choice for kitchen windows. Buy ready-made shades and add your own personal touch or start from scratch to make the shade. Here is one of each to try.

HOW  TO
sew blind ties

1. **Gather** a roll-up blind, fabric for ties, and thread.
2. **For each tie** cut a fabric strip twice the length of the window and about 7 inches wide. With right sides facing, fold each strip in half lengthwise. Using a ½-inch seam allowance and leaving an opening for turning, stitch across the bottom of the strip, up the long edge, and across the opposite end. Turn the tie right side out and handsew the opening closed; press.
3. **Repeat** for desired number of ties.
4. **Loop** ties over blinds and tie into bows.

THE TIE THAT BINDS. *Fabric ties give matchstick blinds designer style.*

HAND-ROLLED. *An elegant toile pattern is showcased on these flat shades. A contrasting fabric on the reverse becomes visible when the shade is rolled by hand. Use this treatment for blinds that will not be raised and lowered often.*

HOT TIP

For a no-sew tie, press each fabric strip under ½ inch on all edges, then press lengthwise with wrong sides together, sandwiching fusible-adhesive tape between the edges to adhere. Or use ribbon instead of fabric ties.

HOW TO

make a hand-rolled shade

1. **Gather** a 1-inch-wide board, paint or stain, decorative fabric, contrasting fabric for lining, staple gun/staples, and four floor-length ribbons.
2. **Cut a panel** from each fabric 1 inch wider and 3 inches longer than the window. With right sides facing and using ½-inch seams, sew the panels together in pairs. Leave the top edge open. Turn panels right side out and press.
3. **Cut the 1-inch-wide board** the same width as the panel. Paint it to match the woodwork. Staple the top edge of the fabric to the board.
4. **Position the ribbons** in pairs—one down the front of the fabric and one down the back—a few inches in from each end of the board; staple them to the back of the board. Roll the board under one turn so the raw edge of the fabric points down; flip one ribbon over the board and one ribbon under it.
5. **Screw the board** to the top of the window frame by working underneath the fabric. Let the fabric hang over the board so the board is concealed. Roll up the shades and tie with ribbons.

personality tiebacks

Add visual "oomph" and the unexpected to kitchen curtains. Try one of these off-the-wall ideas for casual, carefree window treatments.

♦ Dog collars
♦ Nautical rope
♦ Boat cleats
♦ Chain
♦ Strings of seashells
♦ Napkins and napkin rings
♦ Neckties
♦ Empty picture frames
♦ Copper wire
♦ Mardi Gras beads
♦ Pearl necklaces
♦ Coiled phone cords
♦ Holiday garlands
♦ Wreaths
♦ Metal hoops

Most of these tiebacks can be attached to walls with screws or nails. Choose screw or nail sizes appropriate to the sizes of the tieback. For example, choose a smaller nail for delicate pearl necklace tiebacks and longer ones for nautical rope ties. Boat cleats have screw holes for fastening to the wall.

HOT TIP

Anything you can loop around a curtain panel, such as ribbon, rattail cording, rope, or upholstery trim, is a candidate for a tieback. Small objects with holes through them also can be used. Fasten tiebacks to the wall with cup hooks, upholstery tacks, nails, screws, or staples.

THERE'S A HOLE IN MY TEACUP (OPPOSITE). *To copy this look, take cups to a glass store to have 1½-inch holes drilled into the bottoms. Thread a curtain panel through a teacup, playing with the height of the cup. Screw a cup hook into the window frame or wall stud and hang the cup by its handle.*

STAR POWER (LEFT). *Red-painted vintage metal stars (once used as architectural elements on buildings and typically available at flea markets and antiques stores) work perfectly as tiebacks. Hang them on the wall with nails.*

ACCENT walls and floors

You'll love the benefits of accent walls and floors. For one, a painted finish, paneling, or tile conceals less-than-perfect surfaces. For another, some accent materials eliminate worries about splashing water and clinging cooking oils because they're washable.

Cosmetically, accent surfaces break monotony and add pattern to plain places. You can use them to bring focus and vitality to a space. They also add personality and give you a chance to express yourself on large planes. If cabinets cover most of your walls, a backsplash may offer the only opportunity for lively color. You'll find many ideas for them in this chapter.

chicken-print backsplash

Are you an apartment dweller who longs for a country home? You'll love this idea. It goes along with a plan of freestanding kitchen pieces that can move to a larger home when you leave the rental behind. To make an artful backsplash to take with you, follow the instructions below.

HOW **TO**
make this backsplash art

1. **Photocopy images** from an old book on legal-size paper. Buy sets of flexible-glass frames (they're lighter in weight than glass) or ready-made frames. On a paper cutter, cut the images to fit the frame glass.
2. **Sandwich the images** between the sets of flexible glass or in ready-made frames.
3. **Mount** flexible-glass frames on the backsplash wall with photo mounting strips. Hang frames by tapping small nails into the wall.

HOT **TIP**

To find books with interesting images to copy, search used bookstores, flea markets, and online auctions.

CHICK CHIC. Chicken prints nest along the backsplash of this country-style cottage kitchen.

ent
walls and floors

tile backsplashes

Show your style by creatively using tile squares or a free-form mosaic to make focal-point backsplashes. Try one of these processes.

HOW TO

make this rose backsplash

1. **Gather** mesh-back, ¾-inch-square white, red, pink, medium green, and light green ceramic tiles; graph paper and pencil; grease pencil; tile adhesive; white grout; trowel; and sponges.

2. **Chart the backsplash area** onto graph paper with one square equal to one tile. Repeat the rose pattern, *below,* in horizontal rows, alternating the direction and position of the motif between rows.

3. **Use a grease pencil** to mark the placement of the colored tiles. Carefully remove the marked white tiles from the mesh backing.

4. **Apply tile adhesive** to the wall following the manufacturer's directions. Press the mesh-back tiles into place.

5. **Press the colored tiles** into the spaces (refer to the pattern, *below),* making sure they are straight and evenly spaced.

6. **Apply grout** according to the manufacturer's directions after the adhesive dries.

ROSES ARE PINK AND RED. *Easy-to-install mesh-back squares of white tile are the basis for this backsplash technique. Simply pop out a few of the white tiles and replace them with colors to form the rose design.*

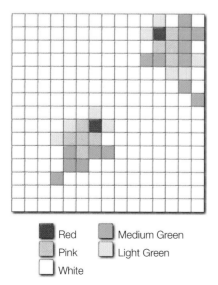

Red   Medium Green

Pink   Light Green

White

HOW **TO**
create a junkyard mosaic

1. **Gather** whole and broken tiles, plates, small flowerpots, snippets of screen, rocks, and marbles. Also collect old terry cloth towels, a hammer, nails, mastic, floor grout, sand, trowel, sponges, and polyurethane.

2. **Leave** some tiles whole. Break up the remaining tiles, flowerpots, plates, and other large items. To safely break the items, wrap them in towels and hit them with a hammer. Lay the pieces on a table or floor to establish a design, rearranging and breaking them again as needed.

3. **Apply mastic** or similar adhesive to the wall and press the mosaic into place. For large or heavy tiles, support them with rows of nails until the mastic dries. Remove the nails and check to make sure the pieces are secure.

4. **Mix floor grout** and thin it slightly with water. Add sand for texture. Apply grout to the wall according to the manufacturer's directions. After the grout dries, seal the mosaic with polyurethane.

DUMPSTER DIVE. A grab bag of tiles, pottery, flowerpots, and found objects becomes a work of art when applied to the wall above this sink.

decor by the yard

Choose your kitchen colors and fabrics with confidence. Use these tips to build your color and pattern courage when creating your own paint-and-fabric wainscot.

▌ **Establish the mood.** If you long for a restful mood, choose wall colors and fabrics in soft blues and greens. If you want an invigorating feel, search out lively reds, oranges, and yellows.

▌ **Collect paint cards and fabric swatches** from paint and fabric stores and take them home to see how they'll look. Do they coordinate well with the furnishings, appliances, and counters? Note how different they look in natural and artificial light as well as in the morning or evening.

▌ **Choose the wall color.** Paint dries darker than it appears when wet. The shinier the finish, the lighter it looks. Wall color is basic to the mood of the room. Once you paint the room, you're ready to shop for wainscot fabrics.

▌ **Shop prepared.** Carry a sample of the wall color with you when you purchase fabrics. Also carry a pre-determined measurement so you know how much of each fabric to buy.

▌ **Buy one geometric and one print** fabric to coordinate with your wall color. Stitch a window curtain to match the wainscot and buy yardage accordingly.

HOW TO
make this colorful wainscot

1. **Measure carefully.** Divide the distance from the chair rail to the baseboard molding into even portions. Determine the fabric square size. (Plan for ½-inch gaps between the fabric squares that allow the wall color to show through.) Determine the amount of yardage needed.
2. **Purchase two fabrics** that coordinate with the wall color in the amount determined in Step 1. Treat the fabric with a spray protector, following the manufacturer's directions.
3. **Cut the fabrics** into squares with pinking shears.
4. **Paste the squares** on the wall, checkerboard style, using a wallpaper adhesive. (Use a level to be sure the arrangement is plumb.) Leave ½-inch gaps between the fabric blocks and skip every third square to allow the wall color to become blocks. Gently press around the edges of the squares to secure them.

HOT TIP

Keep soil and grease off kitchen fabrics by using a spray-on fabric protector. When the fabric is treated, water beads up and brushes away.

PATCHWORK CHARM.
Fabric prints square up on this wainscot wall, giving it a thrifty, homespun look. The squares are protected with a fabric spray.

print walls

Books, calendars, postcards, small posters, photographs, and wallcoverings yield designs you can apply to a backsplash. Photocopies of noncopyrighted material also may be applied.

HOW TO
decoupage a backsplash wall

1. **Prepare walls** by scrubbing, sanding, and wiping them clean. Fill cracks or holes and sand them after the filler dries. Walls should be smooth. Wipe away dust with a tack cloth.
2. **Collect botanical images** from calendars, books, and print collections. If you collect them from various sources and find them in different sizes, be sure they have a similar look.
3. **Trim the prints** to fit your backsplash area; trim away uneven or ragged edges.
4. **Lightly tape the prints** to the wall with low-tack painter's tape, arranging them in stair-step or brick patterns, or at random.
5. **Fasten the prints** to the wall with wallpaper paste or decoupage medium.
6. **Finish** with two coats of clear, satin-finish polyurethane for an easy surface to clean and for moisture protection.

KITCHEN GARDEN. Apply botanical designs clipped from calendars and books to the wall, decoupage style. Polyurethane seals and protects the wall from water damage.

SEASONED TO TASTE. A few well-chosen spice prints go a long way to change the flavor of a room. To help carve a cozy eating area out of a large kitchen wall, this focal-point print arrangement nestles between a plate rail and a wallpaper wainscot.

HOW TO

make a print wall

1. **Gather** prints of seed packets, herbs, and other kitchen-connected images.
2. **Spray** the prints with sealer to protect them from moisture and soil.
3. **Tape** the images temporarily on the wall with low-tack painter's tape as you decide on placement and design, making adjustments as needed. Mark the placement of the images, using a level, ruler, and light pencil marks.
4. **Fasten** the prints to the wall with wallpaper paste or decoupage medium, smoothing out any air bubbles or excess glue with a soft rag.
5. **Frame** a central image with strips of a wallpaper stripe or border. If the wallpaper has a bow design, cut out the bow and fasten it several inches over the center of the print. If not, substitute a ribbon bow.
6. **Attach** a picture hook over the bow and loop a length of chain over the hook. Attach each end to the corner of the print with decorative tacks.

fall for faux— it's cheaper

Paneling that isn't really paneling (see page 13) costs far less than paneling applied to a wall with hammer and nails. The same goes for wainscots that look like wainscots, but aren't. Here's fakery you can practice.

cheap thrills

As an artist with a spirited paintbrush, you're free to decide the height of your hand-painted wainscot. It's part of the thrill of being independent and artistic. Check out these tips while deciding:

♦ The standard height for a wainscot is 36 inches.

♦ Rooms with low ceilings benefit from wainscot heights set slightly lower than the standard.

♦ Large, expansive rooms can be made more comfortable and cozy with a wainscot border set 50 to 60 inches from the floor.

♦ The more checks you paint, the busier the room.

♦ Fewer checks create a quieter, calmer effect.

HOW TO

paint this free-form "wallcovering"

1. **Gather** a satin or semi-gloss latex interior paint in two colors, paint roller and tray, tape measure, carpenter's level, colored pencil in the same color as the paint, clear decorator's glaze, a paintbrush, and a sea sponge.
2. **Paint walls** with the first color (off-white is shown here); let the paint dry.
3. **Mark** every 4 inches along the baseboard and up the walls to the desired height. Using the carpenter's level and colored pencil, connect the marks, creating a checkerboard grid. For a border of rectangles, draw a line 2 inches above the top horizontal line. Draw vertical lines between the top horizontal lines every 1½ inches apart.
4. **Mix** one part of the other paint color (sage green is shown) with four parts of the glaze. Paint alternating squares and border rectangles a few at a time, outlining the shapes with the paintbrush, then using the sea sponge to fill them in. For a mottled look and to add depth to the checks, sponge off some of the paint as you work or add glaze to the paint. Let dry.

CHECK IT OUT. Cook up this painted finish that mimics the look of tile or wallpaper seasoned with a complementary border. You can make the rows of checks go as high or as low on the wall as desired.

tips for floor painting

▮ **Plan your floor painting project** when you have several consecutive days to work on it. While individual steps can be done quickly, the process may take time. Repair and wash your floor before you paint.

▮ **Read paint can labels** to estimate the amount of paint needed. Some cans of paint cover 300 square feet, while some specialty paints cover half that space. You need half as much glaze as paint.

▮ **Keep a supply** of drop cloths and clean rags for protection and cleanup.

▮ **When using rags** for applications or paint removal, use the same kind throughout the project for a consistent effect. Be sure they're clean and lint-free.

▮ **You'll get different effects** with all-cotton rags than with blended or synthetic-fiber rags. Try out the rag, paint, and paint technique on a board to make sure you like the look.

▮ **Remove furnishings** before painting. Remove air vents from the floor.

▮ **Prepare the floor** by cleaning and rinsing it thoroughly. If you plan to paint or stencil over a wood floor that has a glossy finish, sand it first so it accepts the paint better. Pick up the sanding dust with a vacuum cleaner. Then wipe the floor clean with tack cloths to make sure it is lint-free. When the painting or stenciling is complete, protect the decorative effects with a non-yellowing polyurethane.

▮ **Consider the effects of humidity** on your painting. If you're working on a muggy summer day, you'll need more drying time than on a dry winter day.

▮ **Step back** from the floor several times during each technique to look at the surface as a whole and get a sense of composition.

NO-WRINKLE RUG. A two-layer stencil created this rug. The outer and inner border bands are defined with painter's tape and filled in with paint. Leaves are applied over the border one layer at a time.

check out these cheap tricks

Get the look of fancy tiles with paint or jazz up a wall with high-contrast ceramic squares.

PAINT A CHECKERBOARD grid onto large, plain tiles. From across the room, the effect resembles dozens of mosaic tiles applied to a backsplash.

STAMP THE INTERIORS of your cabinets. Glass-front or open-face cabinets can benefit from a square stamp placed on the back walls, checkerboard style. You can buy stamps in crafts supply stores; apply with acrylic paint.

ALTERNATE blue and white ceramic tiles on an accent wall for a striking focal point in your kitchen.

HOW TO

stencil the leaf backsplash

1. **Gather** automotive striping tape, wall paint, leaf stencil, stencil paint, brushes, glaze, brown crafts paint, and sealer.
2. **Create a grid** with automotive striping tape, then paint over the wall with a base coat. (The taped areas become the grout lines.)
3. **Stencil leaves** in various squares and let the paint dry.

STENCIL leaves on a grid of squares painted on a backsplash wall.

4. **Glaze** the backsplash and then use a shading brush dabbed in brown crafts paint and water to add darker edges around the striping tape.
5. **Apply several coats** of sealer after carefully removing the tape. Let dry between coats.

invest in style with paint

With these tips you can accent walls or floors with striping, combing, ragging, and sponging.

■ **Choose the best rollers.** Good roller frames have a compression-type cage with easily removed covers. Natural-fiber roller covers are good for oil-base paints, varnish, or stains. Synthetic-fiber roller covers are best for latex paints.

■ **Protect your woodwork.** Apply low-tack quick-release painter's tape where moldings meet a wall or floor. Easy to remove, it won't leave a sticky residue and costs $3 to $5 a roll at paint or hardware stores. Check labels for levels of tackiness. The best tapes for painted finishes are marked for "delicate" surfaces and promise a clean edge.

■ **Purchase quality brushes.** Choose flat bristles for general painting and angled bristles for trim. To determine the quality, tug on the bristles. If more than two bristles come out, don't buy the brush. You'll pay $6 to $10 in paint stores or home centers for a high-performance brush. For painting with latex and water-base paints, nylon and polyester brushes hold their shape and resilience best. For oil-base paints, a natural-bristle or a synthetic-filament brush works best. A bristle brush has better flow qualities and brushing characteristics than the synthetic-filament brush. It also requires less dipping into the paint can.

HOT TIP

A painted area rug is perfect for a wood floor that isn't in great condition. It helps hide faults, turning a rough, inconsistent plane into a surface rich with color. A painted rug also defines an eating area, turning it into a focal point.

AGED APPEAL. When painting a wood floor, use a light hand to let the beauty of the wood come through. On this kitchen floor, the rug design was applied to bare wood using acrylic paint and taped-off sections of checks. Light sanding creates the well-worn appearance.

STORE to organize

An orderly set of cupboards is a beautiful thing to behold. Organizing and storing kitchen items is just as important as choosing your kitchen's wallcovering or selecting the window treatments.

In this chapter you'll find a variety of storage styles—freestanding, open, closed, decorative, utilitarian, and personal. Some ideas are big, others small. Choose the ones that best suit your needs and the way you use your kitchen.

cookbook library

A handy rolling cart allows you to bring your cookbooks and recipe cards from one food prep area to another. Look for these characteristics when selecting a cart:

▌ **A tall bottom shelf** holds any size cookbook; a short top shelf puts oft-used recipe cards within reach.

▌ **Supportive braces** on the sides and backs of the shelves keep items from falling off.

▌ **A waist-high top surface** makes reading recipes easy. Add a portable cookbook holder to display your working recipe at a comfortable reading angle.

HOT TIP

Adding casters to a shelving unit is another option for a kitchen cart. Be sure the unit isn't top-heavy or tippy and that the casters are strong enough to bear its weight. (Casters have weight recommendations on their packaging.)

LIBRARY CART. This practical cart holds books and boxes. The galvanized metal recipe boxes offer a shiny counterpoint to the darkly stained wicker of the cart.

freestanding storage

A beat-up bedroom dresser is perfect for holding kitchen supplies. Another plus: If it has casters, it moves conveniently around a work space. Try your hand at transforming old-fashioned drawers into freestanding storage to give your kitchen more fun and function.

HOW **TO**
create an antique look

1. **Gather** a blackboard panel, semigloss paint, a towel holder, 12-inch-square ceramic and bullnose tiles (see Step 4), tile adhesive, grout, cup hooks, screws, and new hardware.
2. **Remove** hardware, except for casters. Wash the dresser thoroughly and sand it lightly to ensure a better bond of new paint. Clean with a tack cloth to remove any residue.
3. **Apply** primer. If you plan to add a wooden paper towel holder, attach it now. Apply one or two coats of paint, as needed, to cover the dresser.
4. **Arrange** 12-inch-square ceramic tiles on top of the dresser, adding bullnose tiles around the edges. Some tiles, including the bullnose tiles, will need to be cut to fit. Mark them and take them to a tile shop, where they can be cut.
5. **Secure** the tiles to the dresser with tile adhesive, letting the adhesive dry as instructed on the packaging. Then fill in between the tiles with grout, also following the manufacturer's directions for applying and removing excess.
6. **Screw** in cup hooks for hanging utensils and add new hardware. Attach chalkboard to the back of the dresser by screwing it into place.

PLEASURE ISLAND. *The blackboard on the rear of this re-dressed dresser is used for everything from shopping notes to pint-size masterpieces in chalk.*

HOT **TIP**

If you can't find a chalkboard the right size for the back of the dresser, cut a large chalkboard down to size and surround it with trim. Or cut a piece of medium-density fiberboard (MDF) to size and paint it with chalkboard paint, before attaching it to the back of the dresser.

DRESSED TO THRILL. *A coat of blue paint, a white ceramic tile top, and new hardware bring this old dresser down from the attic to live in the light of this sunny kitchen. Outfitted with kitchen supplies, it delights the eye and busy hands.*

hooks and pegs

Cabinets and appliances take up the bulk of a kitchen's space, but you still can carve out room for stylish storage to hold small items you want to keep handy.

▌**Shaker peg rack.** A familiar solution for hanging coats and hats, shaker pegs also may be useful for hanging utensils.

▌**Pushpin board.** Like miniature pegs, pushpins resemble hooks and are useful for hanging family memos, shopping lists, and calendars.

▌**Magnetic board.** OK, so magnets aren't actually hooks or pegs, but their function is the same. If your kitchen style is utility chic, attach a metal pushpin or magnetic board to the niche above the stove to hold recipe cards, a magnetic timer, and decorative signs.

KEY MEASURES. Team antique rulers with plain metal hooks to hold keys, hats, and dog leashes near your kitchen door.

create this hanging rack

1. **Gather** a nickel-finish 18- to 28-inch curtain rod, two cup hooks, two 1×18-inch fabric strips, needle-nose pliers, and four or five old forks.
2. **Screw** the cup hooks into the bottom of an upper cabinet.
3. **Thread** fabric strips through the hooks and tie the fabric to support each end of the curtain rod.
4. **Bend** forks into hook shapes using needle-nose pliers. In a similar manner, bend tines. (Refer to the photograph, *opposite.*)
5. **Place** forks over the rod; hang utensils, cook mitts, and other lightweight items from the tines.

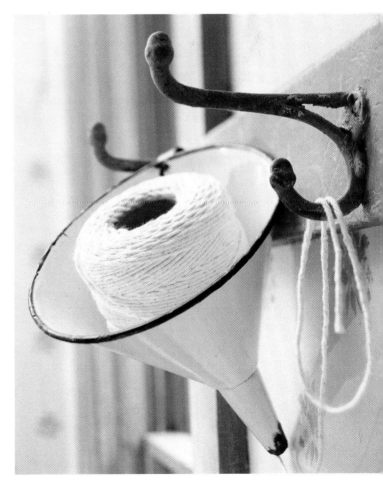

HANGING RACK (OPPOSITE). This system, made from everyday objects, resembles a pot rack hung from a ceiling.

STRING ALONG (RIGHT). Control that junk drawer roll of string with a handy funnel dispenser hung from a peg or coat hook.

where to forage for storage

▌**Home improvement centers** carry the raw materials for designing and crafting shelves yourself (or getting someone to make them for you). The shelves shown are made from plain boards edged with molding and held in place with support rails and shapely brackets cut on a jigsaw. Ready-made wood and metal shelving and hanging systems also are available in home improvement centers as well as at lumberyards.

▌**Garage and yard sales,** junk shops, flea markets, and thrift shops yield surprises—you never know what will turn up. When you shop these sources for shelving or storage pieces, be prepared to think outside the box: Secondhand items can be repurposed into attractive storage containers.

▌**Auctions and estate sales** promise the possibility of finding well-bred or pedigree shelving, cabinets, or hutches at low prices. Attend these events early to snap up the best bargains.

▌**Consignment shops and charitable outlets,** such as the Salvation Army and Disabled American Veterans (DAV) thrift shops, are year-round haunts. Again expect the unexpected. Faithful weekly checking may get you the find or the buy of a lifetime.

SHOW AND TELL. Make room for the objects of your affections. Rather than putting expensive, massive cabinetry over the stove, this homeowner installed simple but stylish open shelving to display her growing collection of cake pedestals.

rescue, renew, restore

Apply "re" to something old and soon it's new again.

▌ **Reclaim.** Save money and furniture lives by rescuing derelicts from junk and salvage stores, garbage trucks, or "as is" racks. Take them home for refurbishing and give them new reasons for being.

▌ **Rethink.** Objects aren't necessarily what they seem. Could that old bookcase be a china hutch or a wall-hung pantry cabinet? See a piece for what it isn't.

▌ **Reinvigorate.** Get out the cleaning compounds, the sandpaper, and the tack cloth. Scrub down this new possibility to within an inch of its life. While you work, make plans for how you'll use it for kitchen storage.

▌ **Repurpose.** View your makeover candidate backwards, sideways, and inside out. For example, an old TV turntable can be topped with a large tray to become a lazy Susan on the kitchen table. Or an outdoor barbecue cart can come inside to be a cookbook library that rolls around in the baking area.

▌ **Renew.** Polish up your adoptee with paint, stain, or fabric. Give it new hardware jewelry. Or perform a facelift on it with paint, ceramics, or a wallpaper pattern.

▌ **Reveal.** Brush away the sawdust, remove the masking tape, and fill shelves to showcase your new storage piece and put it to work.

REPURPOSED. Two unassuming bookcases get china hutch status with a few embellishments: a coat of paint and paper doily edgings hung with double-stick tape along the upper shelves. See detail photograph, below right, for lower-shelf treatment.

REVAMPED. Base cabinets on the lower part of the bookcases are created with fabric panels hung on swing-arm rods.

REVISED (OPPOSITE). These old cabinets didn't seem worth saving until doors came off and the back wall was covered with beaded board. Shelf edgings and faux fronts, cut from pine boards and painted, are glued and nailed in place on the cabinet front.

basket cases

Count the ways baskets make good storage:

1. Easy access. Open shelving organized with baskets is accessible. Without doors to take up space, you can pull a basket quickly from deep shelves.

2. Mobility. By selecting a single basket, you can remove the contents of a shelf and take it to the table or kitchen counter, use the contents without running back and forth, and return the basket when the task is finished. For large, deep shelves, choose baskets with handles.

3. Organization. Baskets on open shelving encourage sorting and categorizing the contents of a kitchen or pantry. If you forget what's in each basket, tie labels to the handles.

4. Inexpensive options. So many choices, so little expense. Galvanized metal or plastic bins and containers are budget- and storage-friendly kitchen shelf alternatives. With plastics you gain washable qualities and a range of colors. White plastics present a vibe of purity and cleanliness, while saturated tones offer zest and energy. Wire baskets are another storage alternative. You can view contents through the walls of unlined baskets, while the liners of wire baskets keep the contents from slipping through.

5. Design. Baskets and bins offer decorative options that emphasize your style. For country or cottage style, the friendly, earthy textures of handwoven baskets are perfect. Galvanized bins lend a utilitarian-chic look to open shelves. Plastic bins and baskets create casual style, and wooden versions with painted designs have a traditional appearance. Be consistent in your basket selection so your lineup has a unified look.

cheap thrills

Inexpensive baskets pop up everywhere:

- ◆ Catalogs
- ◆ Import stores
- ◆ Garage sales
- ◆ Antiques stores
- ◆ Grocery stores
- ◆ Mass-market stores
- ◆ Flea markets
- ◆ Crafts supply stores

PANTRY LINEUP. Coordinated baskets organize staples and produce in this walk-in pantry. For a unified look in open shelving, choose baskets with similar finishes, weaves, and shapes.

storage on wheels

Roll 'em! Some kitchen storage works better on wheels.

▌ **Lazy Susan.** To keep your countertop condiments in line but always accessible, shop garden stores for a plant dolly made in materials to match your kitchen style. A lightweight plastic platter on wheels fits modern work tops; metal or wooden dollies suit traditional ones.

▌ **Mop 'n roll.** Store cleaning supplies in a bucket set on the same style of plant dolly as for the lazy Susan mentioned above. When it's time for a mop-up, nudge the bucket across the floor with ease (no lifting). After cleanup, roll the emptied pail back into the broom closet and re-store supplies in it.

▌ **Pro style.** Shop a restaurant supply store for a sturdy wood-top worktable on wheels. (It'll have great brakes.) Hang a pot rack on the underside of the wooden work top to keep pots and pans handy and visual clutter at a low eye level. (A pot rack hung overhead always has potential for eye-level clutter.)

HOT TIP

Shop mass-market stores for new kitchen carts you can assemble with simple tools. Some quick-assembly wheelies are made for bathroom or laundry room use. But if they're sturdy and good-looking enough, you may bring them into the kitchen as drinks carts or coffee service side tables.

CLEVER CADDY (OPPOSITE). This impromptu bar was devised by outfitting a 1940s kitchen cart with cocktail shakers, mix-and-match glassware, and kitschy bartending books.

PORTABLE WORK TOP (BELOW). A kitchen island on wheels rolls prep space wherever it's needed. The bottom shelf of this refurbished cafeteria cart also offers storage space. It also is a showcase for favorite flea market kitchen finds.

expanding storage

When cabinet storage is short on width, sometimes the only way is up. If you have unused space above stored items inside your cabinets, here's how to get the most out of it.

hang it

▌ **Stemware racks:** Attach inside a cabinet under-the-shelf racks made for wine and water goblets. You'll find ready-made racks in materials to match your decorating style—wood, wire, plastic, or metal.

▌ **Under-the-shelf baskets:** Slide baskets made with long hooks over shelves to make use of the extra space above items stacked on a shelf. Use these baskets to store linens, trays, cleaning cloths, and paper towels.

stack it

▌ **Standing plate racks:** Place a two- or three-tier metal dessert stand on the counter beneath a kitchen cabinet for quick table setting. Instead of desserts, load each level with a stack of plates or wide soup bowls . You'll be able to access them for setting the table or unloading the dishwasher without opening a cabinet door.

▌ **Standing shelves:** Increase your stacking space by placing shelves with legs over stacks of dishes or baskets that sit on your cabinet shelves.

▌ **Baskets:** Collect small items in one basket to keep the clutter down. You'll be able to clean shelves more easily if you can take all the contents down in a single basket.

HOT TIP

Line the space above your cabinetry with baskets so you can store special-use items: table setting decorations, an extra supply of tea lights and candles, and an inventory of cloth napkins.

TOTALLY WIRED. *If you have standard cabinetry above your counter, maximize the space inside with stacking and hanging units. Then apply the same principles to lower cabinets, especially the space under your kitchen sink, to keep cleaning supplies organized.*

small cost, big style

Tableware naturally becomes the art of the kitchen. Utilitarian as well as beautiful, it is best displayed with simplicity and unity. Select your star pieces for a focal-point display.

SHOWCASE SHAPES (RIGHT). *Lineups of white ironstone pitchers, tureens, and teapots show off their best profiles. They add up to gallery-style storage.*

CHINA GALLERY (BELOW). *Plate racks, open shelves, and glass-front cabinets combine form and function in this cozy kitchen. Gallery-white walls show off the dishes' delightful designs.*

TELL YOUR STORY (ABOVE). Spotlight plate patterns by standing them vertically on racks. This narrow glass case fits into a sliver of space and highlights a collection of lovely blue transferware.

GLASS GLOW (LEFT). Glass shelves, custom-cut to fit inside this deeper-than-usual window casing, make a perfect display case for a growing collection of vintage bottles and glass.

storage under glass

In utilitarian kitchens, everyday utensils and ingredients are all the decoration you need. Avoid countertop chaos and shelving clutter by planning a limited, cohesive palette of colors and materials such as clear glass, stainless steel, aluminum, brushed nickel, and white porcelain. Hide other-colored supplies or tools behind cabinet doors and show off your favorite kitchen ingredients under glass.

HOW **TO**
make coffee bean storage

1. **Gather** appealing grocery store jars, such as these spaghetti sauce jars, with screw-top lids.
2. **Spray** the screw-top lids with silver metallic paint.
3. **Screw** the lids to the underside of the wood shelf, allowing enough room between them for easy access.
4. **Print** out coffee bean labels on white paper with your computer.
5. **Cut out** the labels and take them to a print shop for lamination. After they're laminated, trim the labels on a paper cutter, leaving a ½-inch margin around the paper edges.
6. **Punch** holes at the ends of the labels and thread them on kitchen string. Tie the kitchen string around the necks of the storage jars.

HOW **TO**
make a hanging shelf

1. **Buy** one 3-inch-wide and one 5-inch-wide pine or birch boards in the desired length.
2. **Screw** the narrow board to one edge of the wider board to make the hanging rail.
3. **Attach** the shelf to the wall through the front of the hanging rail, inserting screws at stud locations. (Check for studs with a stud sensor.)

UNDERSCORE IT. *Recycled grocery store sauce jars, with their screw lids attached to the underside of a shelf, store a variety of coffee beans. Safety hooks hold cups.*

OVERSIZE IT (OPPOSITE). *Buy oversize jars at flea markets and fill them with similar items for a striking display. Numbers are important for impact, so go for a display of three or more jars.*

DISPLAY your treasures

Kitchen art often is created from useful, everyday items that inhabit your cooking spaces. It's just a matter of knowing how to select a few of them to showcase and to arrange them with skill. Here are tips and techniques that demonstrate how common, ordinary kitchen objects can be raised to the level of high art.

panning for art

To make inexpensive displays, look in these places:

▌ **Your kitchen cupboards.** Do you have large pieces of china that you might enjoy more if they were brought out of the dark and set up on countertop easels? Could you show off a prized collection of copper cooking pots that usually occupies lower cabinets? Do you have a penchant for teapots, salt and pepper shakers, or coffee cups that could be lined up in rows on shelves to show off your personality?

▌ **Your kitchen drawers.** Do you collect utensils or antique tools that could come together in a display on the wall? Do you love balls of string and twine that could be massed together in a large bowl as an interesting conversation piece on a countertop?

▌ **Other rooms of your house.** Which piece(s) of furniture could move into the kitchen and look better there? For example, would those '60s-style plastic/aluminum card table chairs look better pushed up to the breakfast table than they would stacked in the coat closet?

▌ **The garage or garden shed.** Do you see pieces that could be transformed into display racks or containers for small objects? Could you hang kitchen tools on a piece of fencing, create a water feature for the table with terra-cotta pots and saucers, or hang pots and pans from a ladder attached to the ceiling? A new use for an item may occur to you immediately, but if it doesn't, be patient and let its function evolve.

A SLICE OF PIE. Retired pie tins with engraved bottoms make a vintage statement on this kitchen wall. Repeated rows of three achieve balance.

play
your treasures

the artist's way

The best kitchen designers marry form and function. They plan spaces for two kinds of people: those who are cooking and those who are looking. Your decorating style is on display in your kitchen, especially when you decide what to pull together on a countertop.

To arrange a well-designed countertop, remove barely used items. Then sort must-haves by function and organize them in containers. Arrange distinctive bowls or platters on easy-to-reach open shelving, where they'll also serve as art. Edit your counter collection to create a balanced composition and limit the color scheme to one or two colors; add interest with a variety of shapes. Position the largest items first for a backdrop, then layer medium-size objects in front so the arrangement has depth. Overlap pieces to lead the eye across the display but leave comfortable gaps between some items so the grouping doesn't look crowded.

HOW TO
develop your style on a budget

1. **Learn about the elements of good design.** Stroll through art galleries, museums, and fine-furniture and appliance stores. You'll learn to recognize well-designed items when you see them.
2. **Make note of pieces with good proportions** and pleasing lines. You'll soon learn what's good quality and what isn't.
3. **Start a collection** of styles and ideas you like. Collect decorating magazines and tear out pictures that appeal to you. You may discover that you gravitate toward a style: urban, country, traditional, or cottage.
4. **Less is more,** especially when it comes to furnishings. The pared-down approach is elegant and costs less because you don't need as many pieces. Limited numbers of items add the luxury of spaciousness.
5. **Mix and match styles.** The jolt of unusual combinations (vintage with modern or cottage chic with chrome) gives your kitchen a defined style. Plus the eclectic mix-and-match look lends itself to incorporating thrifty finds from junk shops, farm auctions, and other inexpensive shopping venues.

TEAPOT PARTY. Keep cabinets uncluttered by bringing the silver out to shine. A long rod provides support for a focal-point showcase of teapots.

supermarket art

Instead of tossing them out, recycle and repurpose grocery store containers as kitchen displays.

▌ Green-glass bottles. You can't go wrong if you display items that share the same color and material. Create a mini-meadow in a kitchen window with emptied water or vinegar and oil bottles. Vary the glassware heights, from low jars to tall bottles. Arrange the containers in overlapping triangles to create a sense of movement. Stagger pieces from front to back to give the grouping depth.

▌ New salt and pepper shakers, cream and sugar containers, and oil and vinegar bottles from the cookware aisle of your grocery store can become miniature flower vases to place on windowsills or on shelves that need special touches. Consider highlighting a lazy Susan with bright flowers set in a syrup container along with the napkin holder, the sugar bowl, and the salt and pepper shakers. For a successful grouping, choose containers of the same color and style.

SALT SHAKER VASE (ABOVE). Pop a small bunch of flowers from your garden into a salt shaker top, feeding the stems through the holes. Cottage garden flowers such as sweet peas, pansies, and daisies work well.

ARTFUL ARRANGING (OPPOSITE). Spice up the area behind your sink or windowsill with a collection of glass bottles and jars filled with fresh-cut florist blooms or wildflowers.

low-cost ways to display your kitchen treasures

Here are ways to draw attention all around your kitchen.

▍**Walls** can become canvases or backdrops for bold displays. For instance, three cornice-style plate rails mounted on a wall can show off a china collection. To add depth and variety, position smaller items with more vertical shapes along the edges.

▍**An old metal stand** that once held food orders at a diner can be repainted and used to display a collection of antique recipe cards.

▍**Glass bottles** can be arranged inside a pop-out kitchen window. Use bottles of varying heights and shapes. A collection of bottles is more effective if it is limited to one or two colors. If you have a display in one color, stick with the hue's varying lights and darks.

▍**Small shelves** in various sizes can hold interesting items, such as teacups or sugars and creamers. Paint new, unfinished shelves with complementary colors, or collect worn shelves with peeling paint for a vintage look. Home improvement stores offer a wide variety of shelves from $4 to $17.

▍**A timeworn window** salvaged from the curb or a thrift shop can mount on a wall as a frame around a display of plates.

▍**Windowsills** make perfect, no-cost backdrops for collections of small objects, such as miniature chairs or candles.

BALING WIRE (ABOVE), *a part of the Colorado landscape that can be seen from the windows of this kitchen, was used to create this plate rack.*

PLATE RACK (BELOW). *These handmade baling wire plate racks imitate the construction of French spice racks. They run the length of the backsplash.*

recipe card displays

Recipe cards are potential kitchen art. Take a look at your collection. What style do you see there?

▌Humorous. Do you love using blank recipe cards with quirky cartoons? Mount a few on colored mats to make them sturdy enough to hang without curling up.

▌Cozy. Do you prefer cottage-style recipe cards—the old-fashioned kind? They're perfect candidates for the fork easel displays in the photograph, *right*.

▌Utilitarian. Do you file recipes on a computer? Print a few favorites on card stock in your kitchen's color palette with fonts that express your style. (Make cards larger than standard.) Arrange them on a magnetic board from the office-supply store for a utilitarian chic look. (Turn to page 99 for another utilitarian idea for displaying recipe cards.)

▌Sentimental. Do you cook and bake from Grandma's handwritten cards? Do you treasure the recipe cards given you by friends? Get them copied and laminated to assure they last longer.

▌Graphic. Do you get the urge to write recipes on the wall or on a giant blackboard? Give yourself a large wall to record your most-oft-used recipes. You can paint a canvas with blackboard paint, available at paint stores.

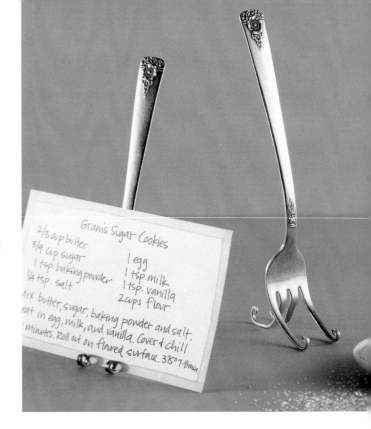

FORK EASELS (ABOVE). *Mismatched flatware often finds its way to a garage sale or a trash can. Old forks make great easels for recipe cards on the kitchen counter, or for photos and postcards as table place settings.*

HOW **TO**
make this metal recipe holder

1. **Determine** the desired length of your holder and add 8 inches. (Make it at least 40 inches long to be flexible enough for mounting on the wall.) The width should be 2 to 4 inches.
2. **Cut a strip** of magnetic metal to size. (Have a metal fabricator do this.) Ask the fabricator to punch a screw hole a couple of inches from each short end. Then bend the metal 4 inches from each end to the back. (The flaps should fit flush against the wall and not be visible when the holder is installed.)
3. **Screw the holder** to the wall (preferably into a stud) through the punch holes, using a drill. Pull the metal away from the wall in a slight curve before you secure it to the wall.

METAL RECIPE HOLDER (OPPOSITE). *Display your favorite recipes on a magnetic holder like this to keep instructions for oft-made dishes within easy reach.*

easy wall art

Turn metal baking dishes into art frames. Different sizes and shapes can hold favorite postcards, photos, or recipe cards. An inexpensive place to shop for baking pans is a restaurant supply store. Many of the pans are oversize so you can frame larger pieces of art.

cheap thrills

Shop the fastener aisles of office supply stores for items you can use to hang small pieces of art in your kitchen. You'll find:

- Magnetic clips
- Magnets
- Giant paper clips
- Pushpins
- Plastic lock-strips
- Money clips
- Binder clips
- Tacks
- Butterfly clamps
- Regal clamps
- Bulldog clips

HOW TO
turn metal baking dishes into picture frames

1. **Gather** metal baking pans, thin cable or picture wire, alligator clips, ferrules (available in hardware sections of home centers), and double-stick mounting tape.
2. **Drill or punch** a small hole at one end of a pan.
3. **Insert** thin cable or picture wire and attach the end inside the pan to an alligator clip (available in the electrical section of a home center or hardware store).
4. **Make** a loop in the end outside the pan and secure with a ferrule.
5. **Repeat** the process on the opposite end.
6. **Fasten** the art between the alligator clips.
7. **Hang** the pan on the wall with double-stick mounting tape.

CLIP ART. Personalize your kitchen by showing off your favorite mementos and collections.

penny-wise displays

▌ **Kitchen vases** come in all sorts of disguises. Check your cupboards for watertight containers. Place small flowers in clear glasses and pretty cups. Consider pitchers and large bowls for a larger bouquet. An upright pottery canister can hold a tall, loose bundle of garden flowers. If the container isn't watertight, insert a plastic or glass liner to hold the flowers. Mass a bouquet of flowers in a lidless pot.

▌ **Candles** clustered on a windowsill, a dreary corner, or on a tabletop lighten the darkness of early winter evenings and create a touch of magic as no other display element does.

▌ **Tabletop treasures.** Display collections that have been hiding in dark storage by bringing them onto the kitchen table or countertop. Massed in a group, antique seltzer bottles, colorful pitchers, or vintage glassware can become personal, yet thrifty centerpieces. For a modern kitchen, consider an inexpensive group of designer-label bottled waters from import stores mixed with water glasses holding fresh flowers.

▌ **Drawer pulls** from flea markets, or home improvement or hardware stores can hold a curtain panel, become pegs for hats and purses on a board, or dazzle cupboard doors with a change. See drawer pulls in objects that aren't intended as drawer pulls. For example, inexpensive porcelain fence insulators can be used as if they were cupboard knobs.

Borrow stylists' display secrets from the pages of decorating books and magazines. One photo is worth a few decorating lessons! You'll find inexpensive and valuable accessory-arranging tips from decorating pros.

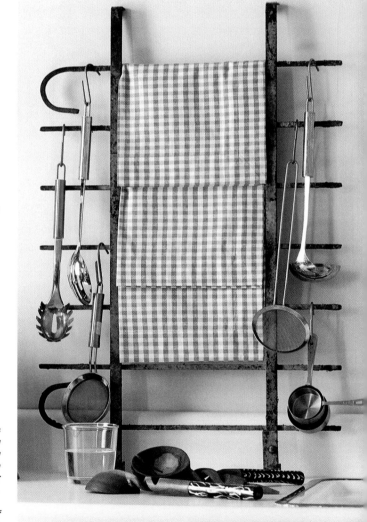

RACK IT (RIGHT). A weathered item like this old iron fencing organizes towels and cooking utensils in a distinctive way. Before using salvaged wood or metal pieces, seal worn paint finishes with a protective coat of clear water-base or oil-base polyurethane.

STACK IT (OPPOSITE). Make the most of your table's real estate by stacking blooms in a tiered plate rack. Tiny field flowers and a draping fern would work equally well on cake stands or candy dishes.

clever ways to add color

Color in your kitchen puts color in your cooking. These tips will put money in your decorating pocket.

▌Paint trim and woodwork. White or off-white paint gives stained woodwork a fresh new look and makes colors in the kitchen appear brighter and cleaner.

▌Add a natural touch. An arrangement of flowers and a large bowl of fruit are easy ways to create quick color. For the greatest impact, make arrangements using a mass of one type of flower or one type of fruit.

▌Group similar colors. Gather like-color items, such as a cluster of plates on a wall, a band of colored-glass bottles in a window, or a gang of red and white salt and pepper shakers.

▌Decide on a color palette. Then select items that complement the palette and display them on a wall, counter, or table.

▌Relocate accessories from adjoining rooms to create a fresh look.

▌Let white or neutral walls become a backdrop for a collection of colorful art or kitchen items from your color palette.

▌Add a rug. A floor covered in a solid light color the same as the wall color makes a room seem to grow. For the opposite effect, use an area rug (especially a dark one) to visually shrink the room by breaking up floor space.

▌Paint the ceiling. For a big impact brush on a color other than white. Pale blues conjure images of summer skies. Pastel peaches overhead feel as rosy as a sunset.

▌Let the sun shine in. One of the newest trends in lighting is using natural light as much as possible. Use light and bright window coverings and keep windows open.

▌Change lightbulbs. Various types of light show color differently. Switching from a tungsten light, which can cast a slightly yellow glow, to a full-spectrum light, which is closer to natural light, brightens a room.

RUSTIC CHARACTER. In a kitchen space that lacks great features, simple touches, such as a distressed-finish chair, a collection of wooden cutting boards, and a blue plate rack filled with brown transferware, add personality and art.

plate-rail drama

Give a blank wall a focal point with this doorless "cupboard" made with painted plate rails and a set of your favorite plates. If you can't find ready-made rails, make your own from materials purchased at a home center.

SLIP NOT. *Use a router to cut a trough in the top of your plate rails. The trough keeps plates from slipping.*

HOW TO
make this plate display

1. **Gather** three 36×1×6-inch clear pine boards (backs), three 36×1×3-inch boards (top rails), wood screws, 10 feet of dentil molding, 12 wooden buttons, wood glue, primer, and white latex paint.
2. **Route** ½-inch-wide plate troughs in the 1×3-inch top rails (see photograph, *right*).
3. **Center** the top rails on the plate rail backs, with back edges flush to each other. Fasten together with wood screws. Use a miter saw to cut the dentil molding trims. Glue and nail them in place under the top rails.
4. **Paint** each plate rail with primer and two coats of white enamel.
5. **Countersink** two sets of screw holes on the faces of the plate rail backs 2 inches in from each end.
6. **Screw** the plate rails to the wall, leaving 12 inches between each rail.
7. **Cover** the screw holes with wood buttons and wood glue. Touch up with paint.

HOT TIP

If you're not a carpenter or inclined toward building these plate rails, substitute antique door headers found in antiques malls and salvage yards. Glue a small molding strip onto the tops of the plate rails to keep the plates from sliding. Tacky wax in front of each plate also works.

BOLD PLATED. *Repetition always delivers, even when subjects are as simple as these plain white plates. Odd numbers of items add up to good design too. Here three rails, each set with three plates function as artwork for this eating area.*

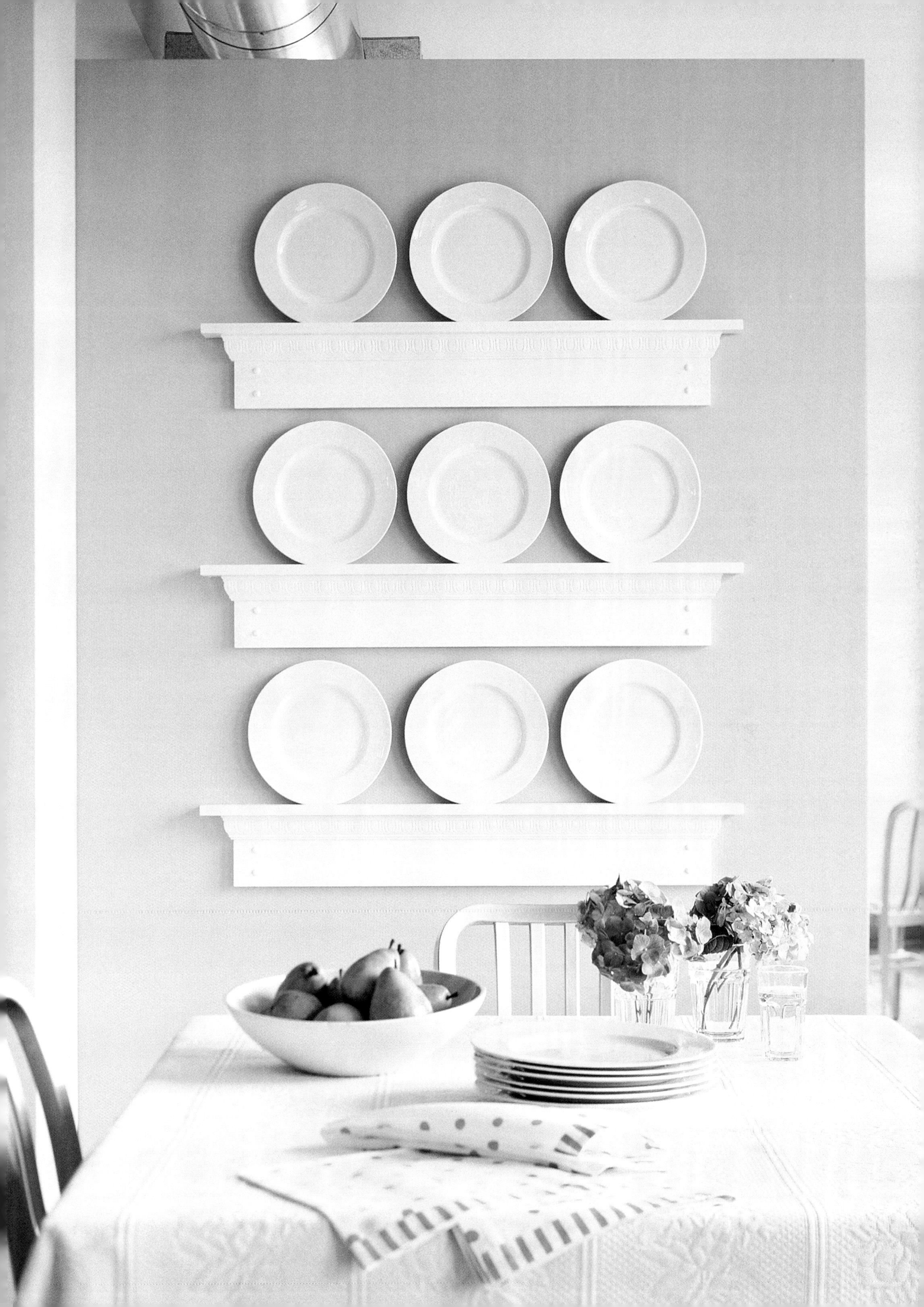

EAT in style

Your breakfast nook or kitchen eating spot is an extension of your kitchen style. Because the average dining room tends to get dressed up for dinner, kitchen dining usually offers more casual options. Often it's the family's most used and comfortable eating spot.

Turn the pages of this chapter to view a variety of popular decorating styles you can adapt to your kitchen and its eating area. At the end of the chapter, you'll find do-it-yourself projects that will add vigor, vitality, and handcrafted style to the place you sit down to eat every day.

farmhouse style

White-wash yesterday's dark and cluttered country ways with today's fresh hues and modern views. White and airy backdrops bring bright rural furnishings into the light.

▌**Paint your kitchen walls, cabinets, and moldings white** to create a clean, white envelope of space. For textural appeal, add a beaded-board backsplash or line open shelving with clapboard.

▌**Choose a table and chairs** with countryside looks. Wingbacks, wicker, or wooden chairs with spindle backs are good choices. For a table, select a square, round, gateleg, or harvest.

▌**Develop a saturated color palette** of grass greens, hydrangea blues, mandarin oranges, and fiery reds. Use the colors on secondhand chairs, tabletop furnishings, tablecloths, dish towels, napkins, and braided rag rugs.

▌**Set the table** with white and bright plain-color china, chargers, vases, pitchers, and bowls. For a step back into the past, light the table in the evening with a lantern or two. Arrange wildflowers loosely in old-fashioned cut-crystal vases.

ATTENTION-GETTER. Gather loved ones at a table surrounded by character-filled chairs in a choice of colors and styles. People gravitate to chairs that suit them.

romantic style

It's easy to produce an open and airy romantic style if you begin with a white-box suburban space, a city apartment with white walls, or an older home that has been whitewashed inside.

▌ **Start with a white backdrop.** If you have to paint walls and woodwork, choose an ivory color that warms the interior while keeping it light. Cover cabinetry with a slightly distressed antique-white finish that goes with ivory walls.

▌ **Choose used furniture** with Victorian lines. Haunt antiques stores, flea markets, secondhand shops, and street curbs for pieces with vintage curves, carved surfaces, and finishes that will look stylish with the same distressed antique white finish you applied to the cabinetry.

▌ **Soften windows** with lace and pastel-color vintage pieces. See the window treatment, *right*.

▌ **Develop a pastel color palette** of lilacs, ivory whites, sky blues, butter yellows, and pinks. Choose printed patterns that carry a base color of soft white. Avoid fabrics and wallcoverings with undertones of beige or tan, which tend to cut back the freshness of romantic color schemes.

▌ **Accessorize with flowers.** The most enjoyable part of putting together a romantic look is finding the right accessories to fill your shelves. In its most energized state, romanticism, like spring, bursts forth in bloom. There is no end to the pretty floral items you can gather for the breakfast nook: painted china and artwork, vintage tablecloths, printed fabrics for seat cushions, dainty tiles and teacups, laces, and flowers.

HANKY PANKY. *Clip old-fashioned handkerchiefs onto a curtain rod covered with a fabric sleeve or a ribbon wrap.*

HOT **TIP**

If you have carpentry skills or know someone who does, assemble a kitchen set by cruising curbs for old furniture on the night before trash collection. Eye the heaps for a tabletop you could pair with another piece of salvage that could serve as a base. Collect mix-and-match chairs to paint or refinish.

SENTIMENTAL WAYS. *Develop a tabletop collection of pinks—vintage tablecloths, pink crystal, floral china, and valentine postcards—to use as table setting surprises.*

HOT TIP

For tropical-style door drapes, make them as long and as loose as possible. For standard 8-foot walls, buy 84-inch-long ready-made sheer panels and undo the stitching on the headers to lengthen them. Open out the fabric, press, and hang the panels from a curtain rod with clip curtain rings. Hang the curtain rod as high on the wall as possible, with the bottoms of the panels about 2 inches off the floor.

island style

Create a carefree tropical island vibe in your kitchen. The look is easy to achieve with these breezy tips:

▌**Blend indoors and out** with sheers or plantation shutters at your windows. Keep your kitchen airy, free of clutter, and open to the view outdoors. If you have a porch, veranda, patio, or terrace just outside your kitchen door, consider that space a decorating opportunity linked to your island-style kitchen. Create outdoor living and cooking spaces that can be quickly covered or stored when bad weather comes. Place lush, green tropical plants near sliding glass doors and windows.

▌**Use tropical hues** on your walls and table. Set the table with white or bright-color china, plastic summer tableware, large trays, glass or plastic pitchers, and wicker chargers. Keep a collection of colorful cotton dish towels, batik tablecloths, and napkins. Use black place mats to set off the bright colors.

▌**Keep window treatments simple.** Avoid fancy hardware and intricate layered looks. Opt for white sheers that contain polyester or other synthetic fiber so you can drop them in the washer, rehang, and allow to air dry. No ironing required! If you have a sliding glass door, soften it at one end with a door drape made from white sheers to blow in the breeze.

▌**Mix natural materials** for a variety of textures. Wicker is a seaside classic, indoors and out. This versatile material can show up in baskets inside or out as storage bins and organizers. Paint wicker chairs for a more formal look. Leave them unpainted to get a rustic feel. Woven straw kitchen mats and sisal, wood, or terrazzo floors are tropical standards.

▌**Accent lighting** that focuses on the table creates a getaway atmosphere. One indoor option is an import-store paper glove on a light cord. Attach it to a corded fixture with a bulb that hangs from a hook in the ceiling and plugs into a wall socket. Another idea: Paint a chandelier white, add colorful shades, and fit it with a dimmer switch. For outdoor dining, hang lanterns from trees to add beauty to meals.

OUTDOOR DINING. If your porch is sheltered from the wind and rain, expand your kitchen eating area by arranging an island-style dining spot outside.

flea market style

A successful personalized kitchen style begins with knowledge of what you love and a sense of how you want your kitchen to feel. If you love vintage objects and want to find everything you need for your kitchen at low prices, flea market style is for you.

▮ **Let your decorating style evolve.** Be patient. Buy one piece at a time, savoring each purchase. Your patient, one-at-a-time purchases will pay off in a distinctive decorating style developed over years.

▮ **Color is key** to a mix-don't-match look. If you have located a key piece, such as a bargain table and chair set like the one shown, take your color cues from it for the rest of the kitchen. For example, the lipstick red of this table and chair set prompts small doses of red in varying amounts throughout the rest of the kitchen. They unify the overall look and color scheme.

▮ **Feel free to mix** flea market styles. Everything doesn't have to be from only one era. For the sake of unity, however, stick to the color palette you've chosen.

▮ **Keep your kitchen walls neutral.** They show off your collections to the best advantage. Like art, your flea-market finds can be hung on walls or arranged in open shelves above or inside your kitchen cabinetry.

HOW TO
negotiate for bargains

1. **Be polite.** Good ways to ask about a discount are: "Is the price firm on this?" or "Is this your best price?"
2. **Use an acting techinque** if you spot something you really love. Don't show too much interest in it, or you may cut your chances to bargain for a lower price.
3. **Don't try to bargain** if a sign says, "Prices Firm."
4. **Ponder buying more than one item** from a dealer, because you could get a better price. It never hurts to ask.
5. **Never make a ridiculously low offer,** such as half. It's likely to annoy the proprietors enough so they'll take nothing off the price.

Flea markets and outdoor antiques fairs can yield a variety of desirable objects, but may be more expensive than other secondhand sources. Don't overlook yard or garage sales. You may find unexpected treasures at rock-bottom prices. Thrift stores, such as those operated by The Salvation Army or Goodwill, also promise good bargains.

RETRO RUSTIC. This lipstick-red table and chairs, priced at only $100, was too great a find for this homeowner to pass up. It inspired her to decorate the kitchen in a 1940s restaurant style.

blue-and-white style

Blue-and-white color schemes may be used in any decorative style—Asian, traditional, country, or modern—and blending blue-and-white patterns is an integral part of setting the table. Here are three print-blending recipes.

▌ The one-color way is the easiest method. First select an overall pattern—a tablecloth—that has a favorite blue printed on or woven into a neutral background. Then find a solid-color runner to alleviate the busy look of the overall pattern. It also highlights an area for arranging dishes that have eye-catching painted patterns. At each place setting, layer plates with simple borders and a pretty center design. Add napkins in various accenting geometric patterns—such as checks and stripes—in the same blue as the tablecloth.

▌ The dominant-print formula means choosing one strong blue-and-white pattern that directs the selection of coordinating furnishings and accessories. Give the dominant print—a wall hanging or a wallcovering—focal-point status. Then select shades or tints of blue from the dominant pattern to echo in painted finishes, small-scale printed fabrics, or china.

▌ The neutral background plan. Reverse the dominant-pattern formula by building a base of neutral solids (see photograph, *opposite*) and gradually working in some patterns. Finish window treatments, some pieces of furniture, and walls in neutrals. Then work in accent patterns with chair cushions, a special paint finish on a tabletop, and ceramic tabletop pieces.

PRINT MIX (ABOVE). This tabletop combines a floral print with solids, simple borders, checks, dots, and stripes.

SECONDHAND STYLE (OPPOSITE). Why spend hundreds of dollars on a kitchen eating area when you can turn an old table set into something special? This eating area has casual Scandinavian charm, thanks to its winning color scheme of cornflower blue, dark blue, and white.

For an Asian-style tabletop, turn a blue-trimmed beach mat into a table runner. Then lay 5-inch squares of origami paper along the runner's edges as a temporary tabletop decoration. You'll find beach mats in import stores and origami papers in art and crafts supply stores.

build-it-yourself style

You will save money and gain style when you pick up a hammer and saw. Wide crown moldings yield perfect ledges for displaying shallow objects, such as photographs, plates, vases, teacups, and salt and pepper collections. Cut boards to fit just below the top edge to securely hold displays.

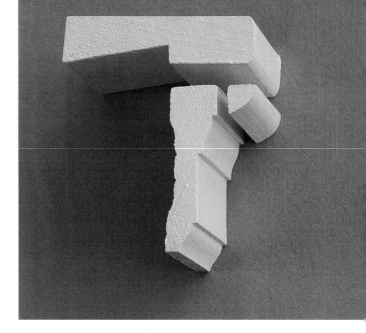

MOLDING MAGIC (ABOVE). *Standard windowsill, colonial casing, and quarter-round molding combine to create these hutch shelves.*

HOW **TO**
build this hutch

1. **Gather** 1×6 poplar boards, windowsill stock, colonial casing, quarter-round molding, screen molding, wood filler, and paint.
2. **Draw** the outside dimensions of the plate rack onto the wall, and wallpaper inside the lines. The bottom of the hutch should be 32 inches from the floor.
3. **Build** the outer frame from 1×6 poplar ripped to 4 inches wide. Cut windowsill stock for the shelves and nail them to the frame, allowing enough space between each piece for the plates you plan to display. Tack a strip of screen molding onto the top of each windowsill piece 2½ inches from the back to make a lip that holds the plates in place.
4. **Mount** the box to the wall by angling screws through the sills and into wall studs. Fill the holes and paint the rack.
5. **Cut** other moldings to fit the length of the windowsill stock shelves and paint them to match. Nail the colonial casing to the underside of each windowsill strip, aligning the back edges. (See detail photograph, *above right.*)
6. **Attach** quarter round to the front of the colonial molding. Paint the chair rail pieces. Mark a horizontal line even with the bottom of the plate rack. Wallpaper the wainscot below the plate rack to this line. Attach the chair rail at the rack base, covering the wallpaper edge.
7. **Fill** the nail holes and retouch with paint.

FAUX HUTCH (OPPOSITE). Using the same wallpaper below the chair rail and within the plate rack carries through the built-in look.

no-sew style

This kitchen gets decorative touches without a needle and thread. A throwback to the 1950s, oilcloth and imitation suede are versatile and durable.

HOW **TO**

make this oilcloth tablecloth

1. **Gather** 1½ yards of 54-inch floral-pattern oilcloth, ¾ yard of 54-inch-wide gingham-pattern oilcloth, a large jar lid, construction glue, and braided, rickrack, or gimp trim.
2. **Cut** gingham-pattern oilcloth into 5-inch-wide strips the same length as the tablecloth edges.
3. **Draw** around half the jar lid to make a scallop pattern on the backs of the gingham-pattern strips, overlapping the scallops so they end evenly at the ends of the strips. Cut out the scallops.
4. **Use** construction glue to attach the strips to the tablecloth. (Note how the scallops meet at the corners in the photograph.) Cover seams with glued-on decorative trim.

HOT **TIP**

For a quick trim around a metal flower bucket, *opposite,* loop orange gingham ribbon into a bow and cut three leaf shapes from green felt. Cut a 2-inch-wide strip of blue gingham. Glue them together with a button on top and secure to the vase with glue.

CUTTING EDGE (OPPOSITE). *These trimmed-out oilcloth pieces are seamed together with glue instead of stitched on the sewing machine.*

CUT IT OUT (THIS PAGE). *Because of its no-fray quality, imitation suede doesn't need hemming. For the chair-back cover, cut two pieces in different colors to desired sizes, leaving the top piece an inch shorter. Cut scallops on each end, following the technique used on the tablecloth, but using a smaller lid. On the top piece of fabric, punch circles in the center of each scallop with a leather punch. Trace a flower stencil on the fabric and cut it out with scissors. Lay both pieces over the chair back and secure grommets where desired. Tie onto the chair back with fabric strips.*

pinstriped pinafore

Dress up your kitchen chairs with easy-to-make slipcovers. Once you make the pattern, you can sew a cover for any season or occasion.

HOW TO
sew this chair slipcover

1. **Gather** medium-weight fabric (the amount varies with the chair height and size), water-erasable fabric marker, and crafts paper for pattern.

2. **Measure.** For the length, start at the rear of the chair and measure from the seat, over the top, down to the seat, and across the seat to the front edge. Add 10 inches to each end. For the width, use the seat width and add 1-inch seam allowances.

3. **Cut fabric.** For side panels, cut two pieces of fabric 10 inches long plus the depth of the chair seat and 1-inch seam allowances. Cut one main panel and two side panels. Hem the short ends of the side panels.

4. **Make** a paper pattern for the front and sides, dividing the panel measurements into three scallops. Turn up a 5-inch hem on each end of the main panel, right sides facing. Transfer the curved line to the bottom of the hem and sew along the line. Clip the curves and trim the seam allowances. Repeat for the back. Turn the hem to the back and press. Make the hemline for the side panels in the same manner.

5. **Place** the main panel over the chair and pin in place. Lay one side panel across the seat, right side down. Align one long edge with the side of the seat cover and pin in place. Repeat for the other side panel. Sew the panels to the cover.

6. **Place** the cover on the chair, wrong side out, to form the upper curve of the cover. Carefully mark the curve of the upper edge of the chair. Sew ½ inch outside the line through both layers of fabric. Turn the cover to the right side and put it on the chair. If the fit is correct, trim away the excess fabric.

7. **Hem** the long edges of the cover, encasing the raw edges. Place the cover over the chair and mark the placement for the ribbon ties. Tack the ribbons in place and tie the cover to the chair.

SIMPLE SLIP. A scallop-edge pinstripe cover resembles a pretty little pinafore. The curves at the bottom are a good match for the shapely rounded top of the chair.

age it with a crackle finish

Give an unfinished hutch, china cupboard, table, or chairs the look and status of a valuable antique with a brand-new finish of paint. You will need crackle medium (available in crafts stores) and paint colors to complement the dining portion of your kitchen. First practice the finish on a board to see how the technique works.

HOW TO
paint a crackle finish

1. **Gather** a primer, acrylic paints in two desired colors, crackle medium (available at crafts or home improvement stores), a clear, water-base varnish, and a practice board (practice the process first).
2. **Sand** the piece of furniture, wall surface, or item you plan to paint. Wipe it clean with a tack cloth and cover it with primer. Let it dry; sand again.
3. **Paint** the surface with the undercoat color. (The bench shown was given a black undercoat.) Let it dry and apply a second coat if necessary.
4. **Apply** the crackle medium to the part of the surface or piece of furniture you want crackled, following the manufacturer's instructions. For fine cracks apply a thin coat; for larger cracks apply a thicker one. Let the medium dry until it's tacky to the touch; when you can leave a fingerprint in the medium, it's dry enough.
5. **Brush** the second paint color quickly over the surface covered with crackle medium. Do not rebrush an area after you apply the paint. (Rebrushing will interfere with the crackling action.) The direction of your brushstroke determines the direction of the crackling. For long cracks that follow the wood grain, make long, straight strokes. To create a web of cracks, apply the top coat of paint with short, slip-slap strokes, brushing in a different direction with each stroke. As the paint dries, cracks will appear. Let the paint dry completely.
6. **Seal** the surface with varnish.

If you find that you really love the crackle-finish look after experimenting with it on a small project, consider applying it to your kitchen cabinetry.

AGED TO PERFECTION. Crackle medium gives a weathered feel to this new bench. Crackling was used only on the seat. Work crackling on part of a piece or finish the entire piece for all-over age and texture.

computer style

Use fabric embellished with iron-on phrases or words to make washable napkins and coverings for kitchen cushions. For phrases, look through books of quotations or consider a line or two from your favorite movie. An optional idea for napkins is to iron on fortune-cookie philosophy.

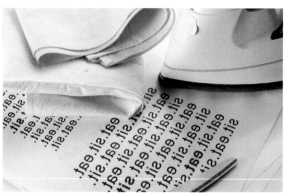

STEP ONE. *Gather materials.*

HOW **TO**

transfer images to fabrics

1. **Gather** transfer images, an iron, the fabric to be embellished (cotton works best), a bedsheet, and scissors.
2. **Cut out** the words or phrases. Turn the iron to its highest heat, with the steam off.
3. **Fold** the sheet and lay it on the ironing board for padding. Set the fabric to be printed on the bedsheet and position the transfer on the fabric. Run the iron over the transfer for several seconds. (Follow the manufacturer's directions that come with the transfer paper.)
4. **Peel off** the backing.

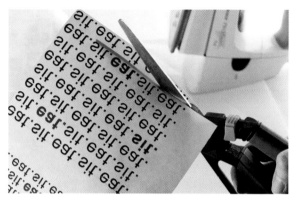

STEP TWO. *Cut out the words or images.*

GET A WORD IN. *Start a conversation at the table with words printed on ready-made napkins.*

STEP THREE. *Iron over the transfer.*

STEP FOUR. *Peel away the backing.*

To create iron-on transfers with words, phrases, or images, purchase computer software designed for printing onto transfer paper. Or photocopy your design onto transfer paper (available at computer and art supply stores). Keep in mind that letters and words need to be printed in reverse to transfer correctly.

SIT ON IT. *Turn printed cotton fabrics into counter stool cushions or chair slipcovers.*

Sit.

decorator's tool kit glossary

If you're the budget-consious type, you like to save on decorating expenses by doing projects yourself. Any project is easier to accomplish if you have the right tools. Here are some basic supplies to keep on hand.

awl An awl, which resembles an ice pick, lets you make a starter hole or pilot hole in wood so nails and screws go in more easily.

can opener You will need this to open a can of paint. Sometimes you can get one free with the purchase of paint. Pick up paint sticks for stirring too.

carpenter's level Don't try to "eyeball" it. Make sure your project is level by resting this tool along the surface. When the item is level, the bubble is centered in the vial. An aluminum level doubles as a straightedge for cutting. Laser levels attach to the wall and shoot a beam of light along the surface, eliminating the need to measure and mark with a ruler and traditional carpenter's level.

caulk It's used for sealing around kitchen sinks and windows as well as for filling gaps between baseboard or crown molding and the wall. Choose a paintable acrylic or acrylic combination for indoor surfaces.

clamps To hold objects together while you work on them or while glue sets, choose multipurpose C-clamps. Use pads when clamping wood to avoid damaging the surface.

crafts knife Check crafts stores for single-blade knives and replacement blades. To get a clean cut when cutting thick materials, such as mat board or foam-core board, use a new blade.

electric drill This tool is indispensable. A ¼-inch drill handles most home decorating projects. Look for a reversible drill with variable speed control. A screwdriver bit makes quick work of installing valances, shelves, and cornices. Cordless drills are convenient if your project isn't near an electrical outlet.

fabric shears These scissors are made for (and should be reserved for) cutting fabric.

floral shears Scissors for cutting flower stems come with notched blades to provide extra leverage when cutting stems and ribbon for bouquets. Some shears can be taken apart for easy cleaning by hand or in the dishwasher.

glues Stock up on a variety of adhesives. For gluing fabrics, check crafts and fabric stores for washable glues. For general-purpose gluing of porous surfaces, such as wood and paper, thick white crafts glue works well. For gluing wood to wood, use carpenter's glue. Five-minute epoxy also is recommended for adhering wood to wood, as well as for gluing nonporous surfaces, including metals, glass, porcelain, tile, and plastic.

grommet tool This tool, which is sold in fabric stores, is designed to press together the two halves of a grommet or eyelet, enclosing the fabric between them and making holes for lacing or threading.

hammer A 16-ounce claw hammer is a good all-purpose tool. The claw provides leverage for pulling nails and removing crooked ones from lumber.

handsaw Quality counts here—an inexpensive saw can chew up your wood and ruin a project. With an 8- to 10-point crosscut saw, you can cut across the grain of the wood, the most common type of sawing. (The points refer to the number of teeth per inch.) A backsaw is a type of crosscut saw with finer teeth (12 to 13 points per inch) for cutting miters. Keep saws covered with a sheath or cardboard when not in use.

hot-glue gun Every do-it-yourselfer needs at least one hot-glue gun. High-temperature glue produces the strongest bond and won't soften when exposed to sunlight or heat. But the glue can burn your skin and damage some fabrics and plastics. Low-temperature glues are less likely to burn skin or fabric, but the glue tends to soften in high-heat areas or in direct sunlight. For greatest versatility, choose a dual-temperature gun that can accept both types of glue sticks; also look for models with built-in safety features.

paintbrushes Choose good-quality natural- or synthetic-bristle brushes for major projects. For small jobs or for use with acrylic crafts paints, inexpensive foam brushes work well and can be tossed out when the project is finished.

painter's tape This low-tack masking tape leaves no residue after removal. Use it to mask off areas where you don't want paint to go while you're painting an adjacent area.

pliers The two basic types you need are slip-joint pliers and needle-nose pliers.

plumb bob Available at hardware stores, this tool is a cord with a pointed weight at one end; it's used to determine whether a vertical line is perpendicular. To use it, attach the end of the cord to the ceiling, suspending the weight just above the floor.

safety goggles Always wear goggles when scrubbing with a heavy-duty cleaner, sanding wood, using furniture stripper, or painting a ceiling.

scrapers Putty knives and scrapers come in different widths for different jobs: removing old paint, wallpaper, varnish, or glue, or applying surfacing compound. Keep them clean and sharpen them often.

screwdriver For the best quality look for cushioned, easy-grip handles and fracture-resistant bars and tips. You need standard and phillips screwdrivers with tips in a variety of sizes.

sewing needles and pins Keep on hand a box of dressmaker's pins, an assortment of sewing needles, and a package of heavy-duty large-eye or tapestry needles. Quilting pins also are good for upholstery fabrics because they're extra long and have large, plastic heads that are easy to see. T pins are heavy, and used for temporarily securing fabric to an upholstered piece.

staple gun This is a must for stapling fabric to a chair seat or to a wood strip for window swags. Look for one that lets you push down at the front where the staple comes out so you'll have leverage.

stud sensor Electronic versions flash and beep when they locate studs, joists, and other objects; the sensor even works through extra-thick walls and floors.

tack cloth Check hardware stores for this loosely woven cloth that has been treated to make it slightly sticky so it picks up sanding dust.

tape measure For sewing projects you will need a flexible plastic or cloth tape with a metal end. For woodworking projects a heavy-duty retractable metal tape is helpful; the end of the tape hooks over a door frame, a window frame, or the end of a piece of wood to hold the tape in place.

window scraper With a single-edge razor holder, you can scrape paint from windows or remove sticky labels from glass bottles and mirrors.

wire cutter This clipperlike tool is handy for cutting mirror- and picture-hanging wire.

HOW TO

store your tools

A designated storage unit saves you both time and money. Hunting down tools is a waste of time that may result in a second purchase that duplicates something you already have, but can't find. If the traditional carpenter's tool chest, fishing tackle box, or antique wood tool carrier doesn't suit your personal style, try one of these creative tool storage ideas:

1. **Look for canvas tool bags** at home centers. Or adapt a hanging canvas clothes holder or a clear vinyl hanging shoe bag. Small- to medium-size tools slip in and out of cubbyholes or shoe slots and are easy to see. If you buy a plastic one, make sure the plastic is heavy and sturdy so sharp objects won't pierce it.
2. **Stackable plastic bins or trays** are other storage options. If you like to carry your tools with you, use a duffel bag or picnic basket. Small, often-used tools can be kept neatly in a cosmetics bag. Or check hardware stores and discount variety stores for specialty tool organizers that incorporate pockets of various sizes and stackable trays.
3. **Assemble a decorating closet**—a space designated to hold practical hammer-and-nail supplies, as well as more creative ones, such as flower vases, candles, or party decorations. It could be a closet at the end of a hall, open shelving in the basement, an armoire with basket containers, a large trunk at the end of a bed, or a space behind a folding screen.

index